Geopolitics of the Indo-Pacific: Emerging Conflicts, New Alliances

by

Kerry Bolton

Geopolitics of the Indo-Pacific:
Emerging Conflicts, New Alliances

by

Kerry Bolton

ISBN-13: 978-1-908476-39-5

Black House Publishing Ltd
Kemp House
152 City Road
London
UNITED KINGDOM
EC1V 2NX

www.blackhousepublishing.co.uk

Email: info@blackhousepublishing.co.uk

Contents

Foreword I

With the growing threat of an American imposition of a sterile commercial world-order, it is not surprising that alternative geopolitical theories such as those of Alexander Dugin, Robert Steuckers and Olivier Védrine have recently gained in popularity. In this context, Dr. Kerry Bolton's book represents a significant contribution to current discussions of the future political, economic and cultural organisation of Asia and Australasia.

In the first chapter Dr. Bolton rightly draws the reader's attention to the dangers presented by America's ally in Asia, China, in its control of the water resources of the Tibetan plateau and in its naval ambitions in the South Pacific. Equally valuable is Dr. Bolton's essay on 'Regional Globalisation,' which highlights the disastrous economic and social consequences of 'economic rationalisation' and the Free Trade principles that have been forced on the world by America since Woodrow Wilson's 'Fourteen Points' and Roosevelt's 'Atlantic Charter' and are propagated today by the Hungarian American Jewish speculator George Soros and his American ally, David Rockefeller.

Far from introducing a harmonious world-order marked by universal economic prosperity, the various American projects only mask a savage economic predatoriness that will erode and eventually eradicate weaker economic and national units. The ambitions of the Americans to cultivate their economic interests through three major international zones, the NAFTA, the EU and the Pacific Asian union stretching from Japan to Australasia are clearly aimed at a unification of the world under their own hegemony. The problem with this American dream is that America does not have the capacity to master even the South American part of its zone, where rival unions such as the Chavez-inspired 'Bolivarian Alliance' have recently arisen. Further,

I

America's pretence of being the leader of the entire 'Western' world is basically belied by the fact that such a leadership can exist only if it succeeds in subverting the entire essentially aristocratic, and anti-American, culture of Europe. Europe's current dependence on the US is linked mainly to its economic organisation as the European Union, but this union is, like all economic ones, already endangered, and further cooperation between Europe and Russia could even break the military hold that America now has over Europe. America's hopes of cultivating an ally in China to contain Russia in the Pacific Asian zone are also not very realistic in view of the fact that China, both as a Communist state and as one allied to American financial interests, is little trusted by the majority of Asian nations.

A rival geopolitical scheme is that presented in the 'Eurasian' programme of the Russian Alexander Dugin, who suggests, in place of an American-ruled world, a multipolar one encompassing an 'Atlantic meridian zone' of the two Americas, a Euro-Africa zone with the European Union as its centre, a Russian-Central Asian zone and a Pacific meridian zone. This is a more classical 'imperialistic' one envisaging Africa and Central Asia as territories that are to be fostered by Europe and Russia respectively. Since, in this scheme, it is not clear if Australasia should belong to the Pacific zone or the Atlantic, Dr. Bolton's own proposal is that Australasia should resist the ambitions of both America and China in Asia by allying itself instead to India and Russia, both of which major powers consider China as their natural enemy while America is, of course, the natural enemy of all.

The alliance of India with Russia is certainly a commendable one since it has not merely a political and economic significance but also a cultural symbolism considering that the ancient Indo-Aryans were originally related to the ancient Slavs. Indeed, viewing matters in historical terms, it will be apparent also that India is naturally suited to serve as a fulcrum of power in Asia because India's sphere of influence in the past extended not only to Hindu-Buddhist South East Asia but also to the Buddhist Far East, including China itself.

On the other hand, it is not certain that Australasia can be considered as anything but a distant appendix of Europe, and especially of Britain. But for such a British-Australasian union to be meaningful the crucial divorce of Britain, as well as of the rest of Europe, from America is a *sine qua non*. And this would entail the replacement of the present American-controlled economic arrangement of the EU with a truly independent European federation.

Given the prevalent folly of admiring 'superpowers' in politics in much the same way that one admires 'celebrities' in society, this book by Dr. Bolton should serve as a timely reminder of the dangers of economically oriented divisions of the world and of the need to cultivate more natural, and longer lasting, associations between culturally congenial nations as a bulwark against the monstrous ambitions of globalists.

Dr. Alexander Jacob

Brno, September 2013

Alexander Jacob is an Indian scholar teaching in the Czech Republic. He received his Ph.D. in the History of Ideas at Pennsylvania State University. He has also worked at York University and conducted research at the University of Toronto. Books include: *Atman: A Reconstruction of the Solar Cosmology of the Indo-Europeans* (2005), *Europa: German Conservative Foreign Policy 1870–1940—Selected Readings* (University Press of America, 2002) among others.

Foreword II

Kerry Bolton defies Kissinger. The latter sees in the Sino-American détente/alliance the head of a spear directed against Russia; and the former brings to light the unique natural ally of Russia—namely India.

Americans today regard the Chinese as the 'people most similar' to themselves; and Bolton explains why: international capitalists' penetration into China (and Tibet), in order to control the natural resources therein and turn the once Celestial Empire into their own Trojan Horse.

Dr. Dimitris Michalopoulos

September 2013

Dr. Dimitris Michalopoulos is a former Lecturer and Assistant Professor, Diplomatic History, University of Salonica (1982–1994); and Professor, Naval and European History, Naval War College of Greece (1989–1997).

Introduction

The 'new world order' that the US imagined would at last be ushered in with the implosion of the Soviet bloc failed to eventuate. The dream of globalist policy-makers and businessmen that the post-Cold War world would grant the opportunity that had been missed in the aftermath of World War II for a monocultural, unipolar global system based upon the cash nexus was soon scuttled—again—by the Russians. Stalin had rejected the US offer after World War II to act as a junior partner in a global regime based upon the United Nations Organization. He had rendered the UN General Assembly useless as a mechanism of world government by his insistence on the veto power of the UN Security Council, and by rejecting the so-called 'Baruch Plan' that would have placed nuclear weapons under 'international' (i.e., US) control. The result was the Cold War.[1]

Into this post-1945 situation two states emerged as powers whose influence will become of increasing importance in the generations ahead: China and India. China soon broke with the USSR, dramatically indicating that geopolitics and national interests take precedence over political doctrines, which are often no more than instruments of *realpolitik*. Historical and ethnographic forces shaped the relationship between China and the Soviet Union, and those same historical forces will continue to impact upon China and post-Soviet Russia. It is the contention of this writer, then, that the present rapport between China and Russia will be no more enduring and has no more historical depth than the supposedly 'fraternal alliance' between Mao's China and the Soviet Union.

---

1   K. R. Bolton, *Stalin: The Enduring Legacy* (London: Black House Publishing, 2012), 'The Origins of the Cold War: How Stalin Foiled a New World Order,' 125–39.

Introduction

It was during the Cold War era that India became a state of significance for superpower geopolitical configurations, sharing with Russia an historical rivalry with China. Again, despite present-day appearances, and talk of 'BRIC,' a Sino-Russian alliance will not endure. The realignment which is already taking place will be one of Indo-Russian alliance vis-à-vis China and the US. The latter continues to regard Russia, under Putin, as its primary obstacle to global influence, despite the comparative weakening of Russia after the Soviet implosion. Hence, old-hand policy-advisers such as Henry Kissinger and Zbigniew Brzezinski continue to see China as a potential US ally in containing Russia, just as they did during the Cold War, and are not so naïve to think that geopolitics can be understood on the basis of such temporary alignments as those between Russia and China. Sino-Russian cooperation is about as durable as the Hitler-Stalin Pact.

Two powers remain global hegemons: China and the US. Russia and the emerging power of India pursue their interests within limited geopolitical spheres. They do not have world-conquering ambitions, either militarily, economically or culturally, in contrast to the US and China.

I write as a New Zealander (albeit one whose views are unlikely to have any significant recognition among New Zealand policy-makers, businessmen or academics) whose nation is being pushed into a nebulous concept known as 'Asia,' and especially in alignment with China, on the basis that it is an economic panacea for an indebted, export-driven economy. There is no such reality as 'Asia' geopolitically, ethnographically, historically, or culturally. There are spheres of common interests within Asia. In the coming generations, crisis scenarios such as drought, flooding, pestilence and famine will instigate the primal urge for survival and conflicts for resources and living space. In particular, conflicts will arise over water resources that will be more acute than those around the security of oil supplies. Hence, the problem of water resources is considered in detail herein. The problem also relates to China's domination of Tibet and its territorial demands on many states from Central Asia to India and Vietnam, and even further afield. So far, China offers the hand of 'friendship' with neighbours because it has been getting everything its own way by negotiation. This expansion by diplomacy will not endure forever.

Such crises will impel new alliances based on geopolitical realities rather than the present questions of trade. Alignments that are more historically organic than artificial constructs based on free trade agreements will emerge by the necessity of survival. An Indo-Russian axis will form the basis of resistance to America's and China's hegemonic ambitions in the Indo-Pacific region, and indeed with worldwide implications. Around such an axis one can expect states such as Vietnam to align. Australia and New Zealand are precariously balanced between the world powers by their exclusive focus on issues of trade. They seek out free trade agreements with Russia, China, the US and India. In doing so, they have placed themselves geopolitically within the orbits of both the US and China. As is shown also by another chapter herein, New Zealand's supposedly solid friendship with the US is also a myth. A final chapter considers alternatives to American and/or Chinese subjugation, and concludes that our place must be within an Indo-Russian alliance.

Background and Overview

The seeming rapport in recent years between Russia and China is one of the foundations of the post-Cold War world. Yet Russo-China friendship is an aberration of history. Even during the 'fraternal friendship' that supposedly existed between the USSR and China, border disputes resulted in the deaths of thousands of Russian and Chinese soldiers, the shelling of Chinese territory, and the desire of the USSR to launch a pre-emptive strike on China to thwart the emergence of a nuclear power. The termination of the Soviet-China treaty that was supposedly the basis of Sino-Soviet collaboration was dramatically signalled by China's invasion of Vietnam. China's past inclination to resort to invasion backgrounds the current suspicion between the two newfound 'friends' amidst China's growing incursions into traditionally Russian spheres of influence.

One of the primary geopolitical shifts in recent years has been the rapport that has *seemingly* developed between two historic enemies, Russia and China. However, the discord between the two powers goes back to the occupation of Russian territory by Mongols for centuries, and the subsequent annexation of Chinese territory by Czarist Russia. This historic conflict was not lessened by the triumph of Communism in China, despite the proclaimed aim of world proletarian solidarity. However, in recent years Russia and China have developed trade and diplomatic relations. Most significantly, Russia has been China's main supplier of arms (followed by Israel). Chinese and Russian leaders sought accord in the face of what they consider US global hegemony following the collapse of the Soviet bloc.

In the 1960s, when Chinese Communists dissolved their 'fraternal relations' with the USSR and resorted to the old ethnic rivalries, American journalist Harrison Salisbury wrote a prophetic book on geopolitics, *The Coming War*

Between Russia and China.[1] Salisbury's predictions seem to have been proven wrong in recent years with the new Sino-Russian accord, yet developments now indicate that his predictions are unfolding, and precisely at the time he foretold they would—the 21st century. Now the diplomat Bobo Lo warns that there is an approaching rivalry between Russia and China, although he stops short to stating that it will become a shooting war.[2] Indeed, much of what Lo states is in broad agreement with the thesis developed in this book; in particular that Russia is closer to Europe and China is closer to the US in a broader view of an emerging 'new geopolitics.' One reviewer, Eimear O'Casey, comments:

> Among the most important points that the author puts forward is that the Sino-Russian partnership is quite firmly of secondary importance to each country's interaction with their respective Western neighbors: Russia with the EU, China with the US. China, says Lo, would choose the US over Russia if pushed. Whilst such an assertion is by nature somewhat speculative, the fact that trade and economic ties between Russia and China are a fraction of ties with the EU and US is a good indicator of its likelihood.[3]

Lo specifies in this regard that the 'Sino-Soviet axis of convenience' is based on 'expediency and opportunism' rather than 'an often illusionary likemindedness.'[4] Russia

---

1   Harrison Salisbury, *The Coming War Between Russia and China* (London: Pan Books, 1969). Salisbury was assistant managing editor of *The New York Times*, and a veteran journalist in Russia and Asia. He was the first American journalist to visit Hanoi during the Vietnam War.

2   Bobo Lo, *Axis of Convenience: Moscow, Beijing and the New Geopolitics* (London: Royal Institute of International Affairs, 2008). Lo was second-in-charge at the Australian embassy in Moscow in the late 1990s and is director of the China and Russia programs at London's Centre for European Reform.

3   Eimear O'Casey, 'China Rising: Bobo Lo: Axis of Convenience: Moscow, Beijing and the New Geopolitics,' AtlanticCommunity.Org, http://www.atlantic-community.org/community-view.

4   Lo, *Axis of Convenience*, 3.

assigns greater resources to the countries of the former USSR and to 'relations with key EU member-states (such as Germany) while China is more focused on relations with the US, ASEAN, the EU and Africa.'[5]

As will be shown below, important political and business circles in the US have always viewed the People's Republic of China as more of an ally than a menace, especially in regard to containing Russia and to providing enormous labour and consumer markets. No other Asian 'ally' can compete with China on either grounds, and therefore all such 'allies' are expendable. As will be seen, just how expendable they are, and how manipulative US policy can be in this regard, will be seen by the manner in which the Republic of China (Taiwan) was discarded.

SINO-SOVIET DISCORD

This writer has long held that a Russo-Chinese accord would not last, but rather that there would be conflict with the possibility of war, stating in an essay privately published in 1983:

> The split between Russia and China over Communist ideology is a mere façade, and practically irrelevant. The real split is historically based. We can trace the Russo-Chinese split back to 1229 when the Mongol 'Golden Horde' of Genghis Khan invaded Russia. The Mongols ruled Russia for 250 years. Even as late as the 18th century Mongols still ruled the Lower Volga and the Crimea. This centuries-long Mongol rule has resulted in an ingrained . . . fear of Eastern conquest.[6]

Harrison Salisbury wrote in *The Coming War Between Russia*

5   Ibid.
6   K. R. Bolton, '*The Washington-Peking-Tokyo Axis: Threat to New Zealand's Survival*,' Wellington, New Zealand, 1983.

and China that 'The Russian makes no distinction between the people of the East. . . . He does not distinguish between the Mongols who ravished his land 600 years ago and the masses of China whom he believes are standing just beyond the low hills of Asia ready to attack again, silently, secretly, without warning.'[7]

Stalin backed Chiang Kai-shek's Nationalists. The primary Soviet goal was a united front between Chiang and Mao to fight the Japanese, while recognising Chiang as the leader of China. Mao put up a pretence of fighting the Japanese and claiming to be able to work with Chiang. Salisbury remarks that Stalin always preferred Chiang to Mao, whom he regarded as a 'Trotskyite.' During World War II Chiang was the focus of Soviet support, not the Reds under Mao. In 1945 the Russians prepared to evacuate Manchuria, but stayed until 1946 at the request of Chiang in order to thwart a Maoist takeover. The Soviet ambassador was only withdrawn from Chiang's entourage on 2 October 1949, the day after Mao announced his Government in Peking. Russia's continuing support for Chiang at the ambassadorial level, right up until the formation of the Communist regime, was a grudge that Mao forever carried. Even under the Sino-Soviet alliance of 1950 the military equipment from the USSR was second rate and expensive. In 1957 Mao took a delegation to Moscow and asked for nuclear warheads, but was rebuffed.

Mao's dreams of establishing China as a superpower rested on the assumption that it would be built up with Russian largesse. This was not the case. Rather the 1950 *Sino-Soviet Treaty of Friendship, Alliance, and Mutual Assistance* that served as the basis of Russo-Chinese relations for thirty years was humiliating and debilitating. It was one moreover which was the primary cause for China's invasion of Vietnam in 1979, as will be considered below.

---

7   Salisbury, *The Coming War Between Russia and China*, 20.

Mao could have cultivated friendship with the US, which was favourable towards a Maoist takeover. General George Marshall, for example, was antagonistic towards Chiang and did not view the Chinese Communists as having Soviet support. Marshall told Chiang that US assistance would halt if Nationalist forces continued pursuing the Red Army into northern Manchuria in 1946 at a time when such an offensive could have finished Mao. This gave Mao a strong base from which to gather his strength and finally defeat Chiang. As Jung Chang and Jon Halliday point out in their definitive biography of Mao, this US assistance to Mao and betrayal of Chiang was decisive.[8]

Conversely, aid from Stalin to Mao was extracted at a very high price; the prelude to the humiliating Sino-Soviet treaty. In return for Russian aid, China was committed to repaying with food on such terms as to create famine. In Yenan, for example, over 10,000 peasants died of starvation. It was a prelude to the future 'Great Famine,' again the price of assistance from Russia.[9]

Mao was determined to establish China as a superpower, but he was badly mistaken if he thought he could secure his ambitions with Russian help. Nonetheless, he courted Stalin by flagrantly repudiating American and other Western relations, although his aggressive action caused Stalin alarm. Chang and Halliday write: 'It is widely thought that it was the US that refused to recognise Mao's China. In fact, Mao went out of his way to make recognition impossible by engaging in overtly hostile acts.'[10]

It is only recently that the secret annexes to the 1950 Sino-Soviet Treaty have become known. The $US300 million

---

8   Jung Chang and Jon Halliday, *Mao: The Unknown Story* (London: Jonathan Cape, 2005), 304–11.

9   Ibid., 310.

10   Ibid., 362.

loan was spread over five years. Stalin approved 50 large industrial projects, many fewer than Mao had wanted. Mao paid a high price in return. Manchuria and Xinjiang were to be recognised as Soviet spheres of influence, with exclusive Russian access to their industrial, financial and commercial activities. 'As these two huge regions were the main areas with known rich and exploitable mineral resources, Mao was effectively signing away most of China's tradable assets.' Mao referred to the two regions among his inner circle as Russian 'colonies.' This was to be a permanent sore point with China's leadership.[11] In 1989 China's leader Deng Xiaoping told Russian leader Gorbachev that, 'Of all the foreign powers that invaded, bullied and enslaved China since the Opium War (in 1842), Japan inflicted the greatest damage; but in the end, the country that got the most benefit out of China was Tsarist Russia, including the Soviet Union during a certain period . . .'[12] Chang and Halliday remark: 'Deng was certainly referring to this treaty.'[13]

The ironically named 'friendship treaty' established virtual Russian colonial status over China. The Chinese had to pay huge salaries to Soviet technicians in China, in addition to extensive benefits to them and their families. Compensation had to be paid to Russian enterprises for the loss of the technicians working in China. The clause that Mao particularly sought to conceal was that which placed Russians employed in China outside of Chinese jurisdiction. The Chinese Communists had always railed against this status imposed on China by the imperial powers during the 19th century as 'imperialist humiliation.'[14] Now the old imperialism had returned under Soviet 'fraternity.'

During the years 1953–54 Mao embarked on a so-called

---

11   Ibid., 368.
12   Ibid., 369.
13   Ibid.
14   Ibid.

'Superpower Programme' that was again to wreak havoc, especially on the peasantry. The Chinese were told that the equipment from the USSR was 'Soviet aid,' implying a gift. But everything had to be paid for, mainly in food.[15] Chang and Halliday state that China has only 7% of the world's arable land but 22% of the world's population, in underlining the seriousness of the Russian terms on China.[16] That is something also which should be kept in mind in regard to present and future developments.

China's repudiation of the Treaty was aggressively signalled by its invasion of Vietnam in 1979 as a direct challenge to the USSR. However, major border clashes and loss of life among Chinese and Russian troops occurred even during the years that the 'friendship' Treaty was operative.

SINO-SOVIET BORDER CLASHES

Sino-Soviet discord through the late 1960s was the result of contention over the status of Outer Mongolia and of numerous territorial disputes along the Sino-Soviet border. These conflicts had festered beneath the surface of Russo-Chinese relations for over a century, since Czarist Russia forced China to sign a series of treaties ceding vast territories. Mao's China considered the USSR as a continuation of Czarist Russia. According to S. C. M. Paine: 'For China, the physical territorial losses were enormous: an area exceeding that of the United States east of the Mississippi River officially became Russian territory or, in the case of Outer Mongolia, a Soviet protectorate.'[17]

The Chinese soon turned their attention to securing the return

---

15   Ibid., 397.
16   Ibid., 398.
17   S. C. M. Paine, *Imperial Rivals: China, Russia, and Their Disputed Frontier* (New York: M. E. Sharpe, 1996). Dr. Paine is an expert on Russia and Asia and has studied in Russia, China, Taiwan and Japan. She is associate professor of policy and strategy at the US Naval War College.

of areas regarded as having been stolen by Czarist Russia. Harrison Salisbury stated that in 1952 a secondary textbook was published, *A Short History of Modern China*, which included a map depicting China with 19th-century borders, designating 19 regions 'lost to a European power.' These regions stretch from India to Indochina. Five other regions were taken by Russia, in addition to Mongolia and Tibet being incorporated into China. Ten years later, China moved on its claims with confrontations on the borders of India, Outer Mongolia and Russia. In 1964, *A Concise Geography of China* was published. This shows China's borders being settled with all neighbours, except for Russia. Frontiers between Sinkiang and Kazakhstan, and along the Amur and Ussuri rivers are designated 'undefined national boundary.' In 1964 Mao told a delegation of Japanese socialists: 'There are too many places occupied by the Soviet Union. . . . About a hundred years ago, the area to the east of Lake Baikal became Russian territory and since then Vladivostok, Khabarovsk, Kamchatka, and other areas have become Soviet territory. We have not yet presented our account for this list.'

In 1960 there were 400 border clashes between Russian and Chinese troops, in 1962 more than 5,000, in 1963 more than 4,000. The biggest clash came on 2 March 1969, when Chinese forces attacked Russian troops on the disputed uninhabited island of Zhenbao (Damansky in Russian) in the Ussuri River. The incident was contrived by Mao as a show of defiance. A Chinese elite unit ambushed Soviet troops, killing 32. The Russians responded on the night of 14–15 March, bringing up heavy artillery and tanks, and firing missiles twenty kilometres into China. Around 60 Russians and 800 Chinese were killed during the engagement. A CIA aerial photograph showed the Chinese side had been shelled so extensively as to look like a pock-marked moonscape. Mao was taken aback by the massive Russian response and feared a Soviet invasion. On 13 August the Russians attacked at the Kazakhstan-Xinjiang border, surrounding and destroying Chinese troops deep inside China. Mao hurriedly ordered defensive earthworks to be constructed should the Russians drive for Peking.[18]

At this time, the Russians intended to drive home their offensive to the point of nuclear attack, but were rebuffed by the US when approval was sought. The journalist Victor Louis, associated with the KGB and Moscow's emissary to Taiwan, stated that Russia intended bombing China's nuclear test site and setting up an alternative leadership structure to take over China.[19] The revelations of a top Nixon aide go further: President Richard Nixon's chief of staff H. R. Haldeman reveals in *The Ends of Power* that the Russians had been warning the US for years that China must not be allowed to develop nuclear weapons. In 1969 the Russians approached the US for a joint strike against China. Nixon rejected the Russian approach, but was informed that they intended to proceed anyway. He warned Russia that the US and China shared common world interests, and would send 1,300 airborne nuclear weapons to Russian cities if Russia attacked China. The Russians backed down.[20] More recent revelations on the 1969 nuclear threat will be examined further in the following chapter of Sino-US relations.

In 1979 the Soviet publication *Soviet-Chinese Relations: What Happened in the Sixties*, stated in a realistic manner the real causes for the Russo-Chinese conflict behind the façade of an ideological rift: 'In analysing the Maoists' stand on the territorial questions, one should turn to China's history and consider the expansionist aspirations of the Chinese emperors and the chauvinistic claims of the Chinese nationalists who dreamed of the return of the "golden age" of the Chinese empire when many of China's neighbours were mere vassals.'[21]

---

18   Chang and Halliday, *Mao*, 570–71.
19   Ibid., 572.
20   H. R. Haldeman, *The Ends of Power* (New York: New York Times Books, 1978).
21   Oleg Ivanov, *Soviet-Chinese Relations: What Happened in the Sixties* (Moscow:

Far from the USSR having been a benevolent father figure in siring a Communist state that would achieve superpower status with Russian arms and technology, and stand side-by-side with the USSR in confronting the imperialist powers and bringing Communism to the world, China had been relegated to the status of a colony.

Towards the end of his life, Mao changed course and sought an alliance with the US, which the American ruling and business elites had long desired. The USSR became the common threat that would be contained by a Washington-Peking Axis. Despite the apparent thawing of the 'cold war' between Russia and China recently initiated by Putin, the main focus for China's power comes from a symbiotic economic relationship between the US and China. This will be considered further.

CHINA'S TERRITORIAL AMBITIONS

China's expansionary aims are not necessitated by the demand for 'living space' or *Lebensraum* in the conventional sense, at least not for the moment, although Salisbury raised the prospect in the advent of a food/population crisis. China has been expanding economically and this has resulted in the movement of Chinese nationals following economic penetration. The advance has been relatively peaceful and subtle, as in the case of the Russian Far East. However, China has in the years since Mao shown itself ready for shooting wars over strategic territory and for shows of force towards its neighbours. Despite the proclamations and treaties aimed at showing China's 'good neighbourliness' towards Russia, Central Asia and India, China stubbornly continues to raise the question of disputed borders in an threatening manner.

One should recall that China invaded Vietnam in 1979 as

Novosti Press Agency Publishing House, 1979), 34.

a grand gesture for the repudiation of the debilitating and ironically named *Sino-Soviet Treaty of Friendship, Alliance, and Mutual Assistance*, signed by Beijing and Moscow on 14 February 1950, which was due for renewal on the day of the invasion. Clause number six of the Treaty stated that if neither signatory announced their intention to terminate the treaty during its final year, the alliance would automatically be extended for another five years. As we have seen, the Treaty was designed not to secure superpower status for China, nor even as a friendly alignment between two supposedly fraternal Communist states, but to maintain a position of subjugation and outright humiliation. The Chinese regarded the Treaty as maintaining Russian 'hegemony' (*sic*) over China. Moreover, the tensions that occurred between Russia and China, including the border clashes resulting in hundreds of deaths and the threat of nuclear confrontation, happened when the friendship treaty was operative. Bruce Elleman states that the 30-year treaty included secret protocols supporting the USSR's role as leader of the world communist movement. He continues:

When Moscow later refused to renegotiate Sino-Soviet territorial disputes, this led to Sino-Soviet border clashes, most importantly during the late 1960s.

Western scholars have all too often overlooked that even during this period of Sino-Soviet tensions, the 1950 Sino-Soviet Treaty of Friendship, Alliance, and Mutual Assistance remained fully in force throughout this entire period of unrest. From Beijing's viewpoint at least, the 1950 Sino-Soviet treaty was a major instrument through which Moscow had tried to exert its 'hegemony' over China.

Moscow was clearly concerned with what might happen when the Sino-Soviet treaty reached its 30-year term. Beginning in 1969, the USSR frequently urged China to replace the 1950 treaty with a new agreement. During 1978, Soviet forces were increased along the Sino-Soviet and Sino-Mongolian borders. Moscow also sought to force Beijing to come to terms by intensifying diplomatic relations with Hanoi, signing a twenty-five-year defense treaty with Vietnam on November 3, 1978.[22]

China's invasion of Vietnam in 1979 was therefore intended as a direct provocation to the USSR, which had signed a defence treaty with Vietnam in 1978, itself aimed at China. This Soviet-Vietnamese alliance made Vietnam the 'linchpin' in the USSR's 'drive to contain China.'[23] The rift between China and Vietnam became apparent when thousands of ethnic Chinese began to flee Vietnam during 1978. Territorial disputes over the Spratly Islands and Vietnam's invasion of Cambodia increased Sino-Vietnamese tensions.

Elleman states that far from China having faced a defeat in Vietnam because of its quick withdrawal, the invasion was aimed at (1) defying the USSR, which had signed a defence treaty with Vietnam, showing the Russians up as so-called 'paper polar bears,' thereby (2) repudiating the Russo-Chinese supposed accord which had been nothing but an encumbrance and was due for renewal at precisely the time of the invasion.

China announced its intention to invade Vietnam on 15 February 1979, the very first day that the 1950 Sino-Soviet Treaty could be legally terminated by either party, and attacked Vietnam three days later. When Moscow did not intervene, Beijing publicly proclaimed that the USSR had

---

22   Bruce Elleman, '*Sino-Soviet Relations and the February 1979 Sino-Vietnamese Conflict*,' 20 April 1996, http://www.vietnam.ttu.edu/vietnamcenter/events/1996_Symposium/96papers/elleviet.htm.

23   Robert A. Scalapino, 'The Political Influence of the USSR in Asia,' in *Soviet Policy in East Asia*, ed. Donald S. Zagoria (New Haven, CT: Yale University Press, 1982), 71.

broken its numerous promises to assist Vietnam. The USSR's failure to support Vietnam prompted China to announce on 3 April 1979 that it intended to terminate the 1950 *Sino-Soviet Treaty of Friendship, Alliance, and Mutual Assistance.*

After three weeks of fighting, China withdrew and disputes over the Sino-Vietnamese border persist. Although China's military action appeared to be a failure, the Soviet failure to respond undermined Russo-Vietnamese relations and 'effectively terminated the Soviet-Vietnamese defense treaty.' 'Thus, Beijing did achieve a clear strategic victory by breaking the Soviet encirclement and by eliminating Moscow's threat of a two-front war.'[24]

China threatened Russia with war if Russia went to Vietnam's aid. Meanwhile, the Chinese had developed an alliance with the US, which threatened the USSR at two fronts. Elleman states:

> To prevent Soviet intervention on Vietnam's behalf, Deng warned Moscow the next day that China was prepared for a full-scale war against the USSR; in preparation for this conflict, China put all of her troops along the Sino-Soviet border on an emergency war alert, set up a new military command in Xinjiang, and even evacuated an estimated 300,000 civilians from the Sino-Soviet border.[25]

China had witnessed a lack of will on the part of Russia, buttressed by the Politburo's failure to act in Poland against Solidarity.

China's imperial ambitions towards Vietnam go back to 208 BC when a Chinese general, Trieu Da proclaimed himself emperor of much of the country. In 111 BC Vietnam was annexed by the Han and became the district of Giao-chi.

---

24 Elleman, op. cit.
25 Elleman, ibid.

Over centuries of resistance some measure of independence was achieved, but Vietnam continued to pay tribute to China. The Mongols were successfully repelled during the 12th century, attesting to the tenacity of the Vietnamese. The Chinese occupied the country in 1407. Liberation was accomplished in 1428 after two decades of further resistance. China attacked in 1788 but was repelled.

In 1909 China tried to claim the Paracel Islands, the start of a series of aggressive moves that continue to the present. In 1956 the Chinese navy took part of the Paracels, with a further invasion in 1974. In 1984 China set up the Hainan administrative area to control the Paracel and Spratly archipelagos. In 1988 Chinese and Vietnamese ships clashed over Johnson Reef. In 1992 there were further incursions into Spratly. The Chinese entered into contract with the US Crestone Energy Corporation in 1994 for the exploration of oil around Spratly; an example of the symbiotic relationship that exists between the US and China economically, behind the façade of occasional superficial differences expressed on the world stage.

In 2000 Vietnam made concessions to China over the territorial waters off Tonkin Bay. During 2004 there were over a thousand Chinese incursions into Vietnamese waters, with 80 Vietnamese fishermen being detained in December. Oil drilling in Vietnamese waters began in 2005. That year the Chinese navy fired at Vietnamese fishermen in Vietnamese waters in the Gulf of Tonkin. In 2007 Chinese fired on Vietnamese fishermen off the Paracels. The Chinese navy conducted exercises in the area. The Chinese Government ratified a plan to build Sansha, a large city to serve as the axis for merging three archipelagos, including the Paracels and Spratly under Chinese control.[26]

---

26   See paracelspratlyislands.blogspot.com

The continuing aggression towards Vietnam by China to the present day indicates that China's 'good neighbour' treaties with Russia, Central Asia and India are expedient masquerades which will drop should China no longer be able to achieve its objectives by diplomatic and subtle means. China covets Vietnam's oil and gas reserves, just as it covets the resources of Central Asia and Western Siberia. Vietnam provides a present-day example of how China reacts when its geopolitical aims cannot be fulfilled other than through war and military coercion.

CHINA'S WAR WITH INDIA

China's border disputes with India during the period of 1960–62 left 3,000 Indians dead. Bill Emmott, former editor of *The Economist* and a member of the globalist think-tank the Trilateral Commission,[27] states of the conflict:

In 1962 China and India fought a border war that humiliated India and left an enduring legacy of bitterness and suspicion. Both countries are now increasing their military spending and trying to modernise their armed forces. The border dispute remains unresolved. China claims an entire Indian state, Arunachal Pradesh, which borders southern Tibet and is roughly the size of Portugal. India claims that China is occupying 15,000 square miles of what is rightfully India—in Aksai Chin, an almost uninhabited plateau high in the Himalayas.[28]

27 The Trilateral Commission was founded at the behest of David Rockefeller, head of the banking and oil dynasty, as a think tank originally based on a merging of interests between North America, Europe and Japan. The concept now embraces the entirety of the Pacific Rim nations. It draws membership from the elite of business and politics. For example the Carter Administration had many Trilateralists, from Carter down. The Commission's first director was Zbigniew Brzezinski, Carter's National Security adviser, who remains an influential voice in US foreign policy, and who is antagonistic towards the rise of post-Soviet Russia as he was toward the USSR. The Trilateral Commission has expanded its membership to China.

28 Bill Emmott, *Rivals: How the Power Struggle Between China, India and Japan Will Shape Our Next Decade* (London: Allen Lane, 2008).

The Chinese are not about to let the disputed areas rest, and again here is a lesson if it is thought that China has repudiated its claims against Russian territory. Emmott states that superficially Indian and China seem to have made progress on the disputed territories, and a border opening for trade was opened in 2006. 'That year, however, the Chinese ambassador to Delhi caused outrage by publicly emphasising that China claims the whole of Arunachal Pradesh. Then a 'confidence building' visit to China by more than a thousand Indian officials had to be cancelled because China 'refused to grant a visa to a member of the Indian delegation from Arunachal Pradesh on the grounds that he was Chinese and did not need one.'[29]

APPROACHING CONFLICT

A recent feature in the *Sydney Morning Herald* based on Lo's assessments shows that the old conflicts between Russia and China are already resurfacing despite the trade relations and the Shanghai Cooperation Organisation. Russia's anxiety trades partly on an old fear that Chinese hordes are itching to take back the resource-rich and under-populated regions of Siberia that Russia annexed from Qing Dynasty China.

> . . . Russia is erecting legal and illicit barriers to Chinese trade in a climate of rising paranoia summed up in the *Pravda* headline: 'Chinese immigrants to conquer Russia.'

> 'The Russians are spooked by the idea you have 110 million people in just three northern Chinese provinces and 6 to 7 million people in the Russian Far East,' says Bobo Lo, author of the forthcoming *Axis of Convenience: Moscow, Beijing and the New Geopolitics*. 'They feel no matter how sweet the political relationship, nature abhors a vacuum and therefore as soon as China feels brave or confident enough to move into the Far East, it will.'

29   Ibid.

Many Chinese traders in Siberia have had to return to China because of new visa requirements and a law that bars non-Russians from making cash transactions in Russian marketplaces.

For their part, Chinese authorities have enforced tough passport requirements on traders who had previously travelled freely across the border. They have also booted thousands of Russians out of northern China as part of an over-zealous security campaign that is driving foreigners out of the country ahead of the Olympics. . . .

. . . Oil volumes fell last year but defence sales crashed, prompting analysts to speculate that China's People's Liberation Army no longer relies on Russian technology. Russia once supplied the bulk of Chinese industrial machinery but now the long lines of excavators, trucks and machinery are all heading the other way.

China is meanwhile increasing its dominance of almost every sector of the Siberian consumer goods market. Two years ago the mayor of Vladivostok made the hyperbolic claim that all of the port city's retail trade and half of its trade in services were controlled by Chinese.

For all the fuss about a Russian-China axis against Islamic separatists and US missile shields, the relationship is constrained by Russian insecurity and Chinese insensitivity. It is just one example of how China's ascendancy is provoking fear and resentment throughout the world and particularly in its immediate neighbours, where the impact is most intense.[30]

The present Russian policy seeks to offset American world hegemony, while her vision of a 'multipolar world'

---

30 John Garnaut, 'Russia on Edge as China Grows,' *Sydney Morning Herald*, 9 June 2008.

does not perceive China as a central factor, despite the development of relations between Russia and China at Putin's initiative. An article in *The National Interest* states of the Sino-Russian relationship that 'Putin's approach toward Asia is heavily influenced by his concerns about the viability of the Russian Far East and Siberia.' Despite Russia's signing of a formal friendship treaty with China in 2000 the Russians remain suspicious of a close relationship with China.'

The Kremlin certainly wants to keep a generally friendly relationship with China and to develop greater economic ties with it. At the same time, it is becoming more worried about the prospect of Chinese migrants settling on the Russian side of the border, thus changing the entire ethnic composition of the region and putting its Russian identity in question. Russia's demographic decline—to the tune of just under a million citizens a year—is a constant theme in Putin's pronouncements. The Russian president is desperately looking for ways to balance against a possibly gathering Chinese threat.[31]

CENTRAL ASIA & THE SHANGHAI COOPERATION ORGANISATION

The basis of the Sino-Russian relationship is the Shanghai Cooperation Organisation (SCO) formed in 1996, first known as the 'Shanghai Five,' bringing together Russia, China and three Central Asian states: Kazakhstan, Kyrgyzstan and Tajikistan, the three countries sharing borders with Russia or China or both. In 2001 the regional arrangement formally became the Shanghai Cooperation Organisation.

---

31 Dmitri Trenin, 'Pirouettes and Priorities: Distilling a Putin Doctrine,' *The National Interest*, 22 December 2003. Trenin is a Senior Associate at the Carnegie Endowment for International Peace and Director of Studies at the Carnegie Moscow Center.

Beijing is the driving force behind the SCO, which allows China to expand its influence in Central Asia. 'Being part of a regional co-operation organisation allows China to portray itself as a responsible good neighbour allowing Beijing to expand its influence without suspicion,' André de Nesnera wrote for the *Voice of America*, citing Bobo Lo.

> The SCO really is China's baby. The SCO allows China to do in Central Asia what it probably wouldn't be able to do at the bilateral level because if China is just dealing with Kazakhstan or Kyrgyzstan, then the smaller state is going to be spooked. But if it's in a sort of a nice pan-regional context, then China can paint itself as a good regional citizen, as a good international citizen and the Central Asians will feel less threatened by them. So the Chinese see the SCO as a way of sanitizing their entry into the region.[32]

De Nesnera writes that although Russia and China are presently in accord over wishing to minimise US influence in Central Asia, both continue to have their own ambitions that are even now coming under strain: 'At the same time, many analysts say Russia still sees itself as the dominant power in the region. Professor Robert Legvold of Columbia University says that for the time being, Beijing and Moscow are deferential to each other,' but 'because of the dynamism and strength and size of the economy, inevitably the shadow of the Chinese economy in Central Asia is growing and being felt by the Russians. And there is an uneasiness in Russia about the sheer magnitude of growing Chinese economic influence in the area.'[33]

Returning to Lo, he states that the present Sino-Russian

---

32 André de Nesnera, 'Russia and China Focus on Central Asia,' Washington, 12 June 2008, *Voice of America*, http://www.voanews.com/english/NewsAnalysis/2008-06-13-voa23.cfm.

33 Ibid.

agreement regarding the countering of the US presence in
Central Asia is not going to obliterate the historical roles both
see themselves playing as the dominant power in the region:

> They have very different visions of what a post-American
> world order and particularly regional order in Central
> Asia would look like. Russia really wants, in a way, to
> return to the old status quo. Now it knows it cannot
> be the old Soviet Union again, so it's not going to try
> that. But it still sees itself as the leading power in the
> region. It has a sort of a sense of historical, strategic
> entitlement. The Chinese, however, think they have just
> as much right to be in the region. So they are actively,
> really actively, pushing their political, security and,
> above all, economic interests in the region.[34]

Lo concludes: 'And Russia and China, in many respects, are
direct competitors.'[35] In *Axis of Convenience*, Lo points out
that the much cited so-called BRIC (Brazil, Russia, India,
China) that is supposedly forming a new geopolitical bloc,
does not negate what he calls the 'trajectory of development'
that 'foreshadows different fates' for Russia and China.[36]

De Nesnera states that analysts will be watching to see what extent
the Russian and Chinese rivalry manifests in Central Asia:
'Most analysts say it will be fascinating to see in the years
ahead the extent of Moscow and Beijing's competition in
Central Asia . . .'[37]

Lo in an interview with a Russian think tank called Open
Democracy explained his perspective on Sino-Russian
relations, which provides further insight.[38] The interview

---

34   Ibid., quoting Lo.

35   Ibid.

36   Lo, *Axis of Convenience*, 7.

37   A. de Nesnera, op. cit.

38   Bobo Lo, 'Russia-China: Axis of Convenience,' 20 May 2008, http://www.

began with the statement: 'The China threat looms large in the Russian imagination, but is not justified by the facts suggests Bobo Lo, writing for OpenDemocracy's new collaboration on Russia and the world.' Regardless as to whether the Russian suspicion of the Chinese is justified or not, it is the perception that matters, and that perception is based on ages-old animosity and the present day grab for resources which could initially become manifest in Central Asia, a pivotal region in geopolitics, and one in which the US and the ubiquitous George Soros[39] have also been particularly active.

Lo has stated as much himself in *Axis of Convenience*, in regard to the importance of perception, which we might call the irrational as the motivating force of history, writing: 'Enduring Russia fears of Chinese irredentism in the Far East highlight the extent to which history still impinges of the relationship, notwithstanding the best efforts of governments to set the past aside.' He states of such driving forces that persist in the Russian psyche that they are attached deeply to the 'idea of land (*zemlya*),' which means that Russian concern at the 'Yellow Peril' invading the Russian Far East will remain.[40]

---

opendemocracy.net/user/511394.

39 George Soros, the currency speculator, operates an array of think tanks, fronts and foundations across the world, aimed at breaking down traditional cultures and opening up protected economies to globalisation. Agendas include liberalisation of abortion and drug laws for example, generally operating under the Open Society Institute, Soros' networks played pivotal roles in undermining the Soviet bloc and are very active in the old Soviet Republics. Soros activities include 'training future leaders' through the 'Internet Access and Training Program' in Belarus, Azerbaijan, Georgia, Kazakhstan, Kyrgyzstan, Turkmenistan and Uzbekistan. Soros networks funded and organised the 'colour revolutions' in Georgia and the Ukraine. Soros is investing heavily in China, along with the other US global corporations. During an interview with the *BBC* at the World Economic Forum in Davos, Switzerland, Soros stated that, 'I'm not looking for a worldwide recession. I'm looking for a significant shift of power and influence away from the US in particular and a shift in favour of the developing world, particularly China.' (*Bangkok Post*, 23 January 2008, http://www.bangkokpost.com/breaking_news/previousdetail.php?id=125401.)

40 Lo, *Russia-China: Axis of Convenience*, 10.

Lo alludes to the accord between Russia and China that was initiated by Putin. However he adds several areas of frustration for the Chinese, one of particular long term significance as to Russian attitudes being that: 'Beijing was also frustrated that the Kremlin cancelled an agreement to build an oil pipeline to China in favour of a Japanese-backed route to the Pacific Ocean.'[41]

Lo does not see this as a long-term problem for Russo-Chinese relations, yet states that this is because China realises that Russia regards herself as a European rather than as an Asian power. This Chinese realisation, based on understanding historical and geopolitical realities, must have a significant impact on Russo-Chinese relations, as it did in the past, even when both nominally shared ideological commitments under Communism. Lo states that Chinese have 'few illusions about Russia,' considering her to be Western-centric. 'That doesn't mean pro-Western, just that Russia looks to the West for its main strategic points of reference. Russia is a European civilisation. Most of its population lives in the European part of Russia. The centres of political and economic power have been always there.' He significantly states that under the Soviet Union the Far East was a 'European outpost, not part of Asia.'[42] Now the Russian Far East is increasingly becoming part of China with a quiet invasion, as demographic changes occur in both powers. We might add that Putin has taken steps to reverse Russia's sharply declining population.

While Lo does not believe there will be war between Russia and China, he nonetheless highlights the underlying tension between the two, influenced by the Russian elite's orientation towards Europe. While Russia wants good relations with China, it is not her primary focus, according

---

41   A. de Nesnera, op. cit., quoting Lo.
42   Ibid.

to Lo.[43] Realism requires one to distinguish what foreign policy analysts generally called 'the West,' headed by the US and centred on NATO, from Europe. 'The West' has since the emergence of the US as the predominant power taking over from an exhausted Europe after two world wars, become far removed from its traditional 'Western civilisation,' and today is an appendage of globalisation of that type that serves US influence, or what the 'Left' has called 'cultural imperialism.' We will briefly consider this globalist consumer culture elsewhere, and the geopolitical significance it is given by US business and political elites, as frankly expressed by Major Ralph Peters for example. Commerce drives US foreign policy; hence, the US is able to have a flourishing relationship with China despite the façade of occasional disagreements on the world stage.

Russia since Peter the Great has existed as a state in which the traditional Russian character, expressed by Dostoyevsky, for example, and in our own time by Solzhenitsyn, has been moulded by the steppes, with a consciousness focused on vast landmasses. Simultaneously Russia has maintained the Petrine[44] aim of technical modernisation based on the Western model. Hence, there is a dual character that is being synthesised and will emerge as something both new and traditional, so long as it is synthesised and does not succumb to the American model. The Russian soul is expressed by Nikolai Berdyaev in *The Russian Idea*:

> There is that in the Russian soul which corresponds to the immensity, the vagueness, the infinitude of the Russian land, spiritual geography corresponds with physical. In the Russian soul there is a sort of immensity, a vagueness, a predilection for the infinite, such as is suggested by the great plain of Russia.[45]

---

43 Ibid.

44 'Petrine': the Westernisation of Russia since Peter the Great.

45 Nikolai Berdyaev, *The Russian Idea* (New York: Macmillan, 1948), 2.

Yeltsin and Gorbachev stood for Petrine Russia, as a colony of 'the West'; Putin stands for Russia *per se*, with its own consciousness expressed by Dostoyevsky, Berdyaev, Solzhenitsyn, et al. This is why foreign policy analysts in the US state in their policy briefings that 'Russia has taken a wrong turn' under Putin, and why NGOs work as avidly to remake Russia as an 'open society' (to use Soros' term) which undermines the Russian soul with the rot of liberalism as the harbinger of commerce. This is why the Duma has recently obliged NGOs operating in Russia to register as foreign agents. As for India, she is not 'Asian' in character, by which is meant Mongolian; she is Indo-European, and like Russia has harnessed Western technology. The danger for both is to be corrupted by the lure of 'Western' commerce and the cultural decay that goes with it, as lauded by Ralph Peters and other zealots of the 'New American Century' when they insist that the fatal attraction of the 'American Dream' is irresistible and will engulf the world.

The historical missions of both Russia and India are distinct and antithetical to the world missions of the US and China. The geopolitical delineations are Russia-India in alliance with other states threatened by both the US and China. As considered subsequently, it is by no means a given that Europe will remain subservient to the US, especially as relations develop with Russia, a prospect that is avidly sought after by Russia herself, and which has precedents in France's own statecraft as epitomised by Charles de Gaulle, who sought friendship with Russia while remaining wary of the US.

Lo is asked: 'Traditionally, the Russians have felt acutely threatened by China. Is that diminishing in the light of the new economic opportunities opening up in the Russian Far East?'[46] Here Lo repudiates the thesis that there will

---

46   A. de Nesnera, op. cit., quoting Lo.

be Russo-Chinese military conflict and the threat of invasion, but rather states that the rivalry will take the form of geopolitical manoeuvring. He sees the 'real threat' from China's rise to be Russia's marginalisation from regional and global decision making. Lo does not believe that a Chinese invasion, even of the Russian Far East, is viable.[47] While it is true that China has been getting all of its own way by diplomatic intransigence, as her neighbours, including Russia, acquiesce, Lo does not seem to be taking into account the rivalry over resources is shaping up even now, a crucial factor that is most clearly explained by Indian analyst Brahma Chellaney.

Yet Lo does not deny the demographics that could see China's excess population seeking *Lebensraum* at Russian expense, as China's population expands and Russia's declines. He states that there are probably more than the commonly accepted figure of 110 million people in northern China compared to fewer than 7 million Russians east of Lake Baikal. 'More generally, we are speaking about a total population of 1.3 billion and rising as against one of 142 million and falling. This clearly plays on the Russian mind.' Lo states that Russians view Chinese far more favourably than previously, however, they remain adamant that they do not want Chinese coming into Russia as labour migrants, they do not want Chinese neighbours; their attitudes remain at street level 'unreconstructed.'[48]

Russia and China 'have very different objectives in Central Asia.' While Russia wants to reassert her regional leadership China aims to be one of three strategic principals in the region, along with the United States and Russia. 'Moscow and Beijing are keen to douse any notion of Sino-Russian rivalry in Central Asia. But this rivalry exists.'

---

47   A. de Nesnera, op. cit., quoting Lo.

48   Ibid.

29

China has done nothing in Central Asia for two hundred years and is keen to get back in the game. But it wants to do this in such way that it doesn't offend others, particularly key states such as Kazakhstan and Uzbekistan. How, then, to package its re-entry so that others do not combine to stop it? The answer is to act under the cloak of pan-regionalism. Here the Shanghai Cooperation Agreement fits in beautifully. It makes China look like a good regional citizen.[49]

China is using the Shanghai agreement as a means of penetrating the region peacefully. Note above that China is comfortable with an American presence in Central Asia. This is very different from the Russian attitude. This would seem to go back to the historical relationships between Russia, China and the US. It seems that again China and the US are in accord in wanting to contain Russia, this time in Central Asia. This is reflected in the contending character of two pacts, that of Shanghai, and that of the Collective Security Treaty Organisation (CSTO), which is fundamentally an anti-China alliance. The Russians understand that Chinese aims are primarily reflected in the SCO. The Russian focus is on the CSTO, which Russia established in 2002. It is significant that China is not a member. The CSTO helps Russia to reassert her influence in Central Asia. 'The SCO and CSTO are effectively competing organizations.'[50]

China's main interest is the stability of Central Asia, where separatism influences minorities such as the Uighurs in China. Hence a US presence in Central Asia would be desirable from a Chinese viewpoint. China's military outreach is directed more towards the Indo-Pacific, which is reflected in the type of weaponry it is amassing, including *Kilo* submarines and *Sovremennyy* destroyers. 'In theory, these might lead not only to the recovery of Taiwan, but

---

49   Ibid.
50   Ibid.

also enable the Chinese to protect the sea-lanes through which 80% of their oil imports pass, and to project power in the South China Sea and the Pacific.'[51]

Hence, one cannot judge the geopolitical realities between Russia and China on the basis of a supposed alliance via the Shanghai Cooperation Organisation. China and Russia both continue to pursue different and rival objectives, bypassing the SCO. However, Russia also regards herself as an Indo-Pacific power, and this has been developing recently.

When Lo states that stability is the principal aim of the Chinese in Central Asia, it appears that he is underestimating the potential for *direct confrontation* between Russia and China, on the assumption that that stability in Central Asia will endure indefinitely, aggravated by a myriad of sources for conflict throughout the entire Indo-Pacific. Lo states that the apparent Sino-Russia accord of the present is uneasy. He states that China seeks to develop 'new sources' for energy in Central Asia. It seems reasonable then to ask whether there will be direct conflict between Russia and China in that region over the question of resources and Chinese incursions presently being undertaken by subtle means? Lo writes:

From the Chinese point of view, greater economic interdependence creates a more stable environment, and energy is the spearhead of this. China worries about the security of sea-lanes. Currently, it gets about 50% of its oil from the Middle East, another 25% from Africa, and the rest from various other countries. It would like to diversify, not just globally but also at the regional level. The Chinese have found it very difficult to develop an energy relationship with the Russians, and they are therefore looking to develop new sources in Central Asia—which is why energy ties

---

51   Ibid.

with Kazakhstan, Uzbekistan and Turkmenistan are so important.[52]

Lo reiterates that he does *not* believe that there will be military confrontation between Russia and China, and alludes to Russian paranoia. Again, this assumes that the insatiability of China in regard to resources, and the potential for major crises in the entire region, will not develop beyond economic rivalry and subtle demographic shifts to actual military conflict. We have already seen border conflicts between Russia and China during the 1960s and 1970s over ancient land disputes, at a time when both supposedly shared a common ideology, and both supposedly stood against the capitalist world. Lo believes that a military confrontation with Russia would be an enormous risk that could bring about the collapse of the regime, however, the gulf between Russia and China will remain, in large part due to differences in psyche. 'Russians like doing business with people they know. They have done gas deals with various European countries since 1967. By contrast, they have little understanding of how the Chinese operate, and doing business with Europeans is more profitable and easier than doing business with Chinese. Russian's focus in its oil and gas lines is on an expanding European market.[53] Oil and gas exports comprise the majority of Russia's exports and total revenue. One could say that Russia and Europe's economies are developing symbiotically in a manner similar to that of China and the US. Lo believes that as China continues to outstrip Russia economically Russia will look increasingly to Europe.

On the other hand, Russian analyst Dr. Andrei Piontkovsky sees Russia and China conflicting in the Russian Far East, and sees this as involving armed conflict. Despite the joint military exercises held by Russia and China, and

---

52   Bobo Lo, ibid.

53   Ibid.

Russia's sale of arms to China, which Piontkovsky sees as short-sightedness by Russia in arming her own enemy, he is dubious about any genuine accord existing between the two powers. Although Russia states that China has peaceably settled her territorial claims with her neighbours, Piontkovsky states that China officially considers several regions in Russia's Far East to be only 'alienated' from it, and these territorial claims are noted in Chinese geography textbooks.[54] He points to China's geopolitical doctrine of 'vital space,' which extends far beyond a state's borders, and includes land, sea, air, underwater and space. This indeed would seem to be in accord with China's strategy which spans the world. China has territorial claims against eleven of its 24 neighbours. 'In China's relations with all of them, the potential use of military force was and remains an important factor.'[55]

Dr. Piontkovsky saw much significance in 'an unprecedentedly large 10-day exercise,' undertaken by China's People's Liberation Army in 2006, involving the Shenyang and Beijing military districts, the two most powerful of China's seven military districts. Shenyang borders the Russian Armed Forces' Far Eastern District, and the Beijing district borders Russia's Siberian Military District. During the exercises, Shenyang units advanced 1,000 kilometres into the Beijing district, engaging in joint war games. Military analysts regarded the Beijing-Shenyang exercises as practice directed toward Russia, since exercises on that scale are undertaken only at the final stage in training for specific strategic and operational plans. 'Such a show of force is an ancient, traditional Chinese political technique.'[56]

---

54   Andrei Piontkovsky, 'China's Threat to Russia,' Project Syndicate, 24 August 2007, http://www.project-syndicate.org/commentary/china-s-threat-to-russia.

55   Ibid.

56   Ibid.

As will be seen in a subsequent chapter,[57] Russia is perhaps not as naïve towards China as Piontkovsky believes, and in 2011 Russia deployed aircraft in the Russian Far East, which was seen as her own signal that behind the smiles and handshakes distrust remains on both sides.[58]

CHINESE ECONOMIC & DEMOGRAPHIC EXPANSION IN THE RUSSIAN FAR EAST

As seen from the above China is pursuing its goals in Central Asia behind a façade of 'good neighbourliness.' The same strategies are being pursued in the Russian Far East. Despite the apparent accord between Russia and China, from high level diplomacy and trade, to commerce of Chinese traders crowding out the markets of the Russian Far East, Putin does not hide his concerns about China. He has long warned of the demographic expansion of China relative to the demographic decline of Russia:

> President Vladimir V. Putin warned last year that the spread of Asian influence in the Russian Far East placed Russia's very existence at stake. 'If we don't make concrete efforts,' he said, 'the future local population will speak Japanese, Chinese or Korean.'[59]

Local authorities also express such concerns:

> 'What we see in the Russian Far East is the peaceful and slow colonization of all Russian territories in the area by the Chinese,' said Alexei D. Bogaturov, the deputy director of the Institute of USA and Canada Studies here. 'We have a grave problem, I think.'[60]

---

57   'Ongoing Tensions.'

58   Ibid.

59   Michael Wines, 'Chinese Creating a New Vigor in Russian Far East,' *New York Times*, 23 September 2001.

60   Ibid.

New York Times correspondent Michael Wines, writing from Zabaikalsk, a town in the Russian Far East sharing a border with China and Mongolia, states of the Chinese encroachment: 'For a lesson in 21st-century geopolitics, come to this border town, until just a few years ago an outpost for Russian infantry awaiting a Chinese invasion.'[61] Russian gun emplacements are crumbling now but the invasion is under way anyway. China builds the new apartments, while China Telecom connects the cellular phones. Chinese traders hire unemployed Russians to sell Chinese-made clothes and electronics through the Chinese-built border crossing. 'The inescapable impression, here and elsewhere in the region, is of a land clinging tightly to its essential Russianness—and slowly losing its grip. Along a stretch of Russian borderland as big as Western Europe, demographics, economics and, for the first time, history are all working against Moscow.'[62]

The collapse of the Soviet Union ended the subsidies the state had provided for the Far East, and the economic collapse has been offset by China, worrying even those Russians who had sought a Russo-Chinese accord to counterbalance the US. The military withdrew for the most part, and towns became derelict. 'From Vladivostok to Zabaikalsk, Russians are coming to depend on the Chinese for everything from buildings to bananas to boomboxes. And that is unsettling even to the architects of the Sino-Russian reconciliation.' Wines states that 'Mr Putin's fear is that Chinese economic expansion will crowd out Russian commerce and political power unless Moscow repopulates and rebuilds this ravaged region first. But precious few Russians want to move here, and money for rebuilding is scarce.'[63]

61   Ibid.
62   Ibid.
63   Ibid.

In a strategy of psychological warfare aimed at wooing Russians into embracing Chinese overlordship, the Chinese have built a model city, albeit one that does not reflect the reality of the Chinese peasant. This is strange behaviour for a state to undertake towards a supposed strategic ally and seems more reminiscent of the Communist propaganda that was broadcast across borders and fields to Cold War enemies. From Zabaikalsk 50 yards across the border, 'past abandoned Russian tanks and rusted barb-wire fences,' China has built a free trade centre of hotels, freight-forwarding offices, wholesale stores and pagodas.

> On the horizon, 10 minutes down a freshly paved highway in China, is the city of Manzhouli. Ten years ago a Chinese version of Zabaikalsk, it is today a staging area for Russian trade—a forest of skyscrapers and cafes 'where even the street sweepers have cellular phones,' one Russian said enviously. 'It's a beautiful city. I wish ours was like that,' said a Russian woman who would identify herself only as Valentina.[64]

What more glaring example can there be that China has designs on Russian territory that have not diminished? The land, oil and other resources of the Russian Far East beckon. Chinese farmers presently rent and cultivate land in the Russian Far East due to the shortage of land in China. In the Primorsky Krai[65] region some 30,000 Chinese have permanent residence. The region is a disputed territory, with rich land that was not cultivated until the arrival of Russians in the beginning of the 17th century. Treaties in 1858 and 1860 moved the Russian border south to the Amur and Ussuri rivers, giving Russia possession of the region, which was to become a site of conflict during the 1960s and 1970s.

---

64   Ibid.

65   Russian Maritime Province.

Primorsky Krai's economy is the most successful in the Russian Far East based on food processing and in particular fishing. The annual catch constitutes one half of the Russian Far East total. Agriculture includes the production of rice, milk, eggs, and vegetables. The breeding of livestock, especially sheep, is well developed. The timber industry has an annual yield of about 3 million cubic meters and is the second largest in the Russian Far East. Machine manufacturing is the second most important component of the economy, with half of the output servicing the fishing industry and shipyards. The construction materials industry supplies the whole Russian Far East. The region generates more electricity than any other Russian Far East administrative division. 'The defence industry is also important; with naval vessels and military aircraft production. The railway infrastructure is twice the Russian average, and is connected with China and North Korea. The coastal location makes the region an important maritime trade and defence route into the Pacific. Primorsky Krai-based shipping companies provide 80% of marine shipping services in the Russian Far East.'[66] Primorsky Krai is the largest coal producer in the Russian Far East. Among the other minerals found here are: tin, tungsten, lead, zinc, silver, gold, fluorspar ore (containing rare minerals such as beryllium, lithium, tantalum and niobium), and Russia's largest supply of boron ore (boron being used in textiles, aerospace materials, smelting, control of fission in nuclear reactors, rocket fuels, jet engines, and hundreds of other uses).[67]

As the Russian Far East becomes increasing reliant on Chinese investment, while the Chinese population expands and the Russian declines, a future food-population crisis in China could see the Russian Far East as China's *Lebensraum* to be taken by force. Primorsky Krai is a rich prize in both

---

66   Primorsky Krai, http://en.wikipedia.org/wiki/Primorsky_Krai.

67   Boron, http://en.wikipedia.org/wiki/Boron.

land and minerals. Tibet was invaded, colonised and turned into a 'special economic zone' by China for the control of the many mineral resources there and the water sources for much of Asia. In any one of a number of crisis scenarios that could afflict China and Asia generally, the Russian Far East would be irresistible.

The *Daily Telegraph* reported in 2009 the Russian ethnic population decline in the Russian Far East, in comparison to the burgeoning Chinese population across the border, coupled with the tremendous mineral resources of the area. David Blair writes that 'the vast swath of territory between Lake Baikal and Vladivostok may become a new theatre of confrontation between Russia and China in the decades ahead . . . The empty lands of the Russian Far East, far closer to Beijing than Moscow, contain major sources of tension between the two powers.'

> . . . The quest for raw materials is the central goal of [China's] foreign policy. And virtually every natural resource imaginable is found just over the border. Here, beneath steppe and tundra, are large reserves of natural gas, oil, diamonds and gold, while millions of square miles of birch and pine provide immense supplies of timber. All this amounts to an astonishing combination: a densely packed country trying to keep its economy roaring ahead by laying its hands on natural resources, living alongside a largely empty region with huge mineral wealth and fewer inhabitants year on year. Russia and China might operate a tactical alliance, but there is already tension between them over the Far East. Moscow is wary of large numbers of Chinese settlers moving into this region, bringing timber and mining companies in their wake.[68]

---

68   David Blair, 'Why the Restless Chinese are Warming to Russia's Frozen East,' *Telegraph.uk.co.*, 16 July 2009, http://www.telegraph.co.uk/comment/5845646/ Why-the-restless-Chinese-are-warming-to-Russias-frozen-east.html.

Blair believes that Russia might be obliged to turn to the US for help in resisting Chinese expansion into the Russian Far East. His error is fundamental in seeing a rivalry that would bring the US and China together vis-à-vis Russia. In the following chapter on 'Sino-American Relations,' we shall examine the historical relationship between the US and the People's Republic of China.

TREATY WITH MONGOLIA AIMED AT RUSSIA

China still sees Mongolia as an integral part of its territory, and has long been coveted by China. Mongolia's historic relations with Russia have been to offset Chinese hegemony. However, China has in recent years displaced Russia in Mongolia, which was previously a Soviet protectorate. China is pursuing its integration of Mongolia via diplomatic means. The friendship treaty with Mongolia is aimed at Russia. China underlines the strategic importance of Mongolia for both itself and Russia: 'As China's important neighbor to its north, and situated between China and Russia, Mongolia enjoys a unique geographic position. . . .'[69] The Chinese Foreign Ministry describes the relations between China and Mongolia when the latter was under the Soviet umbrella as having suffered 'ups and downs':

> In 1962, both sides signed Sino-Mongolian Treaty on Friendship and Mutual Assistance, and in 1962, signed the Boundary Treaty. In mid and late 1960s, their relations suffered ups and downs. In 1970s, the two countries restored to exchange of ambassadors. In 1980s, their relations saw gradual improvement.

> In 1987, China and Mongolia restored scientific and technological exchanges suspended for more than the previous 20 years, and signed the 1987–1988 Plan for

---

69 Ministry of Foreign Affairs, Peoples Republic of China,
    http://chinese-embassy.org.za/eng/wjb/zzjg/yzs/gjlb/2742/default.htm.

Scientific and Technological Cooperation.[70]

The Ministry's statement on Mongolia has details about the cultural, economic and educational relations between the two, but merely mentions in passing 'development in the military area.'

> In 1989, their state and ruling party (Chinese Communist Party and Mongolian People's Revolutionary Party) were relations normalized. Since then, their friendly relations and cooperation have consolidated and developed in such areas as the political, economic, cultural, educational and military. In 1990, China and Mongolia issued a joint communiqué, revised Sino-Mongolian Treaty on Friendship and Mutual Assistance in 1994, and signed Friendship and Cooperation Treaty between China and Mongolia based on the previous treaty. . . . China is now Mongolia's largest trading partner and investor. Both sides share identical or similar views on many issues in international affairs, support each other and enjoy fruitful cooperation.[71]

The Soviet control of Mongolia was secured under the humiliating 1950 Sino-Soviet treaty. Elleman states that Soviet control of Mongolia was one of the ongoing contentions between Russia and China. In 1950 Mao grudgingly recognised the 'independent status' of the Mongolian People's Republic, i.e., Mongolia's status as a protectorate of the USSR. 'This admission was a far cry from recognizing Mongolia's complete independence from China, however, since Mao firmly believed that the Soviet government had earlier promised to return Mongolia to China. Based on Mao's later complaints, Mao must have received assurances from Stalin that Mongolia's status,

---

70 Ministry of Foreign Affairs, Peoples Republic of China,
    http://chinese-embassy.org.za/eng/wjb/zzjg/yzs/gjlb/2742/default.htm.

71 Ibid.

as well as the exact location of the Sino-Mongolian and Sino-Soviet borders would be discussed at future meetings.' When the USSR refused to negotiate, clashes occurred between Russia and China at the Mongolian border during the 1950s and 1960s. Although the Sino-Mongolian border was resolved in 1962, Mao publicly denounced Soviet encroachments on Chinese territory and protested against Soviet control of Mongolia, stating that the Soviet Union, 'under the pretext of assuring the independence of Mongolia, actually placed the country under its domination.'[72]

Mongolia has remained contentious between Russia and China even after Mao's death. In 1978 the Chinese were still demanding Russia's withdrawal from Mongolia, despite the wishes of Mongolia herself for the protection accorded by Russia. On 26 March 1978, China's Ministry of Foreign Affairs demanded that the USSR recognise the existence of 'disputed areas' along the Sino-Soviet border, completely withdraw Soviet troops from Mongolia and pull back from along the entire Sino-Soviet border.[73] The USSR responded by increasing Russian defences along the disputed borders, while Mongolia reiterated its friendship with Russia and hostility towards China:

> In response to China's demands, Leonid Brezhnev, the General Secretary of the CPSU Central Committee, visited Siberia during early April 1978, and announced that new, more advanced equipment had been provided to missile units stationed along the Sino-Soviet border. These new weapons, Brezhnev announced, would be instrumental in 'securing ourselves and our socialist friends against possible aggression, whatever the source.' Soon afterwards, on 12 April 1978, Ulan Bator also publicly protested Beijing's demands, stating that additional Soviet troops had been stationed along the

---

72   Elleman, op. cit.

73   Ibid.

Sino-Mongolia border at Mongolia's request in order to offset increased Chinese troop concentrations to the south of the border.[74]

In 2006, Russia and China offered to build railways, using different tracks running in opposite directions, running from the Tavan Tolgoi mine, one of the world's largest unexploited coal deposits,[75] indicating the rivalry that continues.

Elsewhere, border disputes between China and Kazakhstan from the Soviet era have been replaced by the two coming closer together, again with Russia being sidelined from this oil- and gas-rich state.[76] Russia's traditional sphere of influence in Afghanistan was dislodged by an alliance between the US and what are now referred as 'Islamists,' who nonetheless remain useful pawns in extending US interests worldwide on the pretext of the 'war on terrorism.' While Russia was eliminated from Afghanistan, under the US occupation regime China has moved in to gain vast oil and gas concessions in northeast Afghanistan. Bhutan is regarded as a buffer between India and China and while aligned with India, diplomatic accord with China has not been extended, nor has a disputed 495 square km been resolved.[77]

China has been pursuing policies in regard to her neighbours through economic subversion, from which is now proceeding a silent invasion of Chinese, populating Russian territory and displacing Russia in Mongolia through Chinese economic clout. This is the same strategy that China is using throughout the South Pacific, extending its influence over the small but strategically situated island nations through aid and economic development, followed

---

74 Elleman, ibid.
75 Ibid.
76 Ibid.
77 Ibid.

by the opening or buying of port facilities.

Mongolia, like Tibet, is rich in minerals. Its wealth includes coal, copper, molybdenum, iron, phosphates, tin, nickel, zinc, wolfram, fluorspar, gold, uranium, and petroleum. It is a prize that has been lost by Russia. While China's neighbours acquiesce to China's demands, which having been proceeding step-by-step, there remain many outstanding disputed areas:

- Aksai Chin in the disputed territory of Kashmir, at the junction of Pakistan, Tibet, and India. India claims the 38,000-square-kilometre territory, currently administered by China.

- Arunachal Pradesh, a state of India, bordering on Bhutan, Bangladesh, Myanmar, and China. China calls the 90,000-square-kilometre area South Tibet.

- The Senkaku Islands, five unpopulated islands in the East China Sea, which are under Japanese control. China and Taiwan both claim them, calling them the Diaoyutai Islands and Diaoyu Islands, respectively.

- Portions of China's western border with Tajikistan.

- A section of the boundary between China and North Korea in the Baitou Mountain area.

- The Paracel Islands in the South China Sea, administered by China, but claimed by Vietnam and Taiwan.

- Rich fishing rights and oil reserves of the Spratly Islands in the South China Sea, claimed by China, Taiwan, Malaysia, the Philippines, and Vietnam.[1]

---

1   'Border Disputes in China,' CBC News, 19 April 2005, http://www.cbc.ca/news/
     background/china/borderdisputes.html.

Russia's dispute with China centred around the control of Zhenbao Island (Damansky in Russian) on the Ussuri River and islands on the Amur and Argun rivers. These disputes led to shooting conflicts during the 1960s. Russia's compromise with China, now supposedly settling all disputes with China in regard to boundaries, included Russia handing over half of Heixiazi Island (Bolshoy Ussurysky Island), at the confluence of the Amur and Ussuri rivers, to China in 2004.[2] China can well regard itself as a 'good neighbour' when it gets everything its own way, softly-softly, with occasional forays into disputed territories with 'gunboat diplomacy' when those neighbours start getting complacent.

---

2   Wenwen Shen, 'China and Its Neighbours: Troubled Relations,' EU-Asia Centre, 1 March 2012, http://www.eu-asiacentre.eu/pub_details.php?pub_id=46.

The Sino-American Relationship

There are some who, for varying reasons, would appease Red China. They are blind to history's clear lesson, for history teaches with unmistakable emphasis that appeasement but begets new and bloodier war. It points to no single instance where this end has justified that means, where appeasement has led to more than a sham peace. Like blackmail, it lays the basis for new and successively greater demands until, as in blackmail, violence becomes the only other alternative.—General Douglas MacArthur, 1951.[3]

What of the US factor in Indo-Pacific and Sino-Russian affairs? Will the US step in and confront China, which is often seen as a geopolitical rival in its ambition to secure ports and waterways around the world? Would the US confront China in a showdown over Taiwan? Would the US, perhaps in alliance with Russia, confront Chinese incursions into Central Asia? Any confrontation between the US and China is unlikely. In a confrontation between Russia and China the US will not intervene against China any more than the US was willing to assist Russia in preventing China's gaining nuclear capabilities.

The US attitude is unlikely to have changed from 1982 when US National Security Adviser William Clark told Australian Prime Minister Malcolm Fraser that Australia 'would be expected to cope alone with any local or regional conflict.' The exception would be if the USSR were supporting an aggressive state. But China was regarded as an ally against Russia.[4] In 1983 Paul Wolfowitz, more latterly US Deputy Secretary of Defence and president of the World Bank, when US Assistant Secretary for East Asia and Pacific Affairs, told Chinese Premier Zhao Ziyang that the US

---

3   General Douglas MacArthur, Farewell Address to Congress, 19 April 1951.
4   *The Dominion* (Wellington, New Zealand), 29 May 1982.

'welcomed China's increasing and stabilising influence in the region, which he described as one of the more dramatic recent shifts in power play in south-east Asia.'[5] Over the course of several decades since 1983, the role of China has certainly been far more 'dramatic.'

When Mao repudiated the 1950 'friendship treaty' with Russia, signalled by the invasion of Vietnam, he sought an alliance with the US. This was the culmination of a long-desired aim of political and business elites in the US, particularly those associated with the Rockefeller banking and oil dynasty.

Jung Chang and Jon Halliday state that Mao had sought an alliance with the US as far back as 1953, when Stalin died. However, the Korean War had made such a relationship impossible to sell to the American people. In 1969 President Nixon expressed interest in pursuing relations with China.[6] It was at Korea that the US was directly confronted by China. The reaction was a telegram from the Joint Chiefs of Staff advising General MacArthur to prepare to evacuate and leave the peninsula to the Communists. As the document shows, the US was well aware that China had directly entered the conflict.[7] General MacArthur considered the American policy 'defeatist' and made four recommendations:

(1) Blockade the coast of China; (2) destroy through naval gunfire and air bombardment China's industrial capacity to wage war; (3) secure reinforcements from the Nationalist Chinese garrison in Formosa to strengthen our position in Korea if we decided to continue the fight for that peninsula; and (4) release existing restrictions

5   *The Evening Post* (Wellington, New Zealand), 3 May 1983.
6   Jung Chang and Jon Halliday, *Mao: The Unknown Story* (London: Jonathan Cape, 2005), 601.
7   Joint Chiefs of Staff telegram to General Douglas MacArthur, December 1950.

upon the Formosa garrison for diversionary action against vulnerable areas of the Chinese mainland.[8]

President Truman responded to MacArthur's opposition regarding a 'no-win' policy—a policy that was to be repeated in Vietnam—by dismissing the popular military commander in 1951. Much has changed since that time, but the changes make a direct confrontation between the US and China even less likely: China is now dealing from a position of strength far beyond its capabilities in 1950, and in particular the economies of China and the US are now in symbiosis. Any military confrontation would have repercussions more far-reaching globally than MacArthur's recommendations in 1950.

SINO-SOVIET-US RELATIONS AND THE 1969 NUCLEAR THREAT

In 2010 the news media came out with a Chinese exposé showing that in 1969 the USSR wished to settle its historical score with China and launch a nuclear attack. The USSR merely wanted an assurance of US neutrality. Far from the US welcoming this declawing of the growing dragon, the US instead threatened that there would be retaliation against Russia. According to a report first carried in the *Daily Telegraph*, Chinese historian Liu Chenshan, writing in an officially sanctioned newspaper, stated that the threat 'came in 1969 at the height of a bitter border dispute between Moscow and Beijing that left more than one thousand people dead on both sides.'[9]

Liu quoted Soviet premier Alexei Kosygin as stating to Soviet leader Leonid Brezhnev on 15 October that

---

8   General MacArthur to the Joint Chiefs of Staff, December 1950.

9   Andrew Osborn and Peter Foster, 'USSR Planned Nuclear Attack on China in 1969,' *Telegraph.co.uk*, 13 May 2010, http://www.telegraph.co.uk/news/worldnews/asia/china/7720461/USSR-planned-nuclear-attack-on-China-in-1969.html.

'Washington has drawn up "detailed plans" for a nuclear war against the USSR if it attacked China.' The *Telegraph* speculated that Liu is likely to have had access to official archives given the appearance of this as part of a series of six articles in an official news source. The *Telegraph* article continues: 'The historian claims that Washington saw the USSR as a greater threat than China and wanted a strong China to counter-balance Soviet power. . . .' It concludes: 'Mr Liu, the author, admits his version of history is likely to be contested by rival scholars.'

However, this Chinese revelation was not 'new' to informed observers. The Russian desire to settle scores with China came amidst the culmination of border disputes that had been ongoing since 1960. The USSR intended to drive home their offensive with a nuclear attack. Chang and Halliday refer to an article at the time published in a London newspaper 'by a KGB-linked Russian journalist Victor Louis,' who had been Russian emissary to Taiwan, stating that the Kremlin was discussing bombing China's nuclear test site, and planning to set up an 'alternative leadership' for the Chinese Communist Party.[10] Moreover it was US President Richard Nixon's aide H. R. Haldeman who seems to have first broken the nuclear attack story in his memoirs in 1978.[11] He stated that for years the USSR had been trying to warn the US against allowing China to become a nuclear power. Haldeman's claim seems to directly contradict Liu's claim that Nixon, when responding to the 1969 Soviet request for neutrality, did so not only because he regarded China as a means of containing Russia, but also because he was still 'smarting from a Soviet refusal five years earlier to stage a joint attack on China's nascent nuclear programme.'[12]

---

10   Chang and Halliday, *Mao*, 572.

11   H. R. Haldeman, *The Ends of Power* (New York: New York Times Books, 1978).

12   Osborn and Foster, 'USSR Planned Nuclear Attack on China in 1969.'

If we place this all into context, the 1978 Haldeman version is more likely than that of Liu's present contention. If the US had asked for support from the USSR to bomb China's nuclear facilities in 1964, this was a year following Sino-Russian border conflicts resulting in 4,000 dead. In 1960, there had been 400 clashes; in 1962, 5,000. The USSR would have no sentimental, comradely, ideological, diplomatic, or geopolitical reasons to oppose such a US proposal and then change her mind five years later and make a similar suggestion to the US.

The relationship between China, the US, and the USSR is quite contrary to how it is generally perceived. A more accurate scenario is that the US backed Mao and the USSR backed Chiang Kai-shek. Stalin, prior to Mao's assumption to power, regarded him as a Trotskyite. While Stalin had previously backed Mao as a counter to a Trotskyite coterie in China,[13] by 1938 Mao was being denounced in the USSR as a Trotskyite.[14]

During World War II, while the US was pushing Chiang to make an alliance with Mao against the Japanese, Stalin was counselling Chiang against this.[15] General George Marshall warned Chiang in 1946 at a crucial time that if he persisted in pursuing the beleaguered Red Army into Northern Manchuria, American aid would stop. This provided Mao with a base from which to recuperate and finally defeat Chiang. On the other hand, Stalin's aid to Mao was granted according to Russian interests as distinct from Communist fraternity, one particularly dramatic example of which was the demand for repayment in food that resulted in over 10,000 peasants dying of starvation in Yenan.[16] This was a prelude to the debilitating *Sino-Soviet*

---

13   Chang and Halliday, *Mao*, 75.

14   Ibid., 216.

15   Ibid., 304–11.

16   Ibid., 310.

Treaty that was to result in the 'Great Famine' for the same reason.[17]

Mao thought that he could make China a great power on Stalin's coat-tails. This was a grave error. While the US attempted to court China, Mao went out of his way to act 'Bolshie' towards the 'Paper Tiger,' in a futile effort to court Stalin. Chang and Halliday write: 'It was widely thought that it was the US that refused to recognise Mao's China. In fact, Mao went out of his way to make recognition impossible by engaging in overtly hostile acts.'[18]

Given the historically strained (at best) relationship between China and Russia, even at a time when they were supposed to be ideologically aligned, what are likely future scenarios on the world stage? There seems to be a preponderant view that the US and China will increasingly become rivals due to economic and raw material factors. There is also a view that the US and Russia will align against China.

PRO-CHINA BIAS OF US ESTABLISHMENT

Influential interests in the US have a long-term vested interest in China, and an almost innate distrust of Russia from Stalin's ascension to power onward.[19] As with the Bolshevik Revolution during Woodrow Wilson's time,[20] the US 'foreign policy establishment' was by no means hostile to a Communist takeover of China. Despite Mao's forlorn hope of Stalin's comradely patronage, the 'foreign policy establishment' and big business interests centred on the Rockefeller axis never gave up on China. While General

---

17 Ibid.

18 Ibid., 362.

19 K. R. Bolton, *Stalin: The Enduring Legacy* (London: Black House Publishing, 2012).

20 K. R. Bolton, 'Lessons from America's Intervention in Russia 1918–1920,' *Foreign Policy Journal*, 13 January 2011, http://www.foreignpolicyjournal.com/2011/01/13/lessons-from-americas-intervention-in-russia-1918-1920/.

MacArthur was removed in 1951 for wanting to act against China's intervention in the Korean War, in 1953, the year of Stalin's death, Mao sought an alliance with the US. However the war made such an alliance impossible to sell to the American people.[21]

It was 1970 when the long-awaited rapport with China could be broached publicly; the year following Nixon's threat to retaliate should the USSR try to take out China's nuclear programme. The ubiquitous Henry Kissinger, a lifelong protégé of the Rockefeller dynasty, paved the way. That dynasty had been eyeing China since the 1920s. In 1956, John D. Rockefeller III founded the Asia Society to promote business relations with Asia. In paying tribute to Kissinger at the 50th anniversary banquet of the Asia Society, Richard Holbrooke stated:

> To discuss the Rockefeller Legacy, not just John D. Rockefeller III, but the whole family, there really was only one person who could do it, and that was Henry Kissinger. Henry has been a friend of the Rockefeller family as you all know, Vice President Nelson Rockefeller, David Rockefeller, and the rest of the family, so many of whom are here tonight, for fifty years. He also has a very strong and deep connection to Asia. We all know that he was the main architect of the historic opening to China, which has resulted in so many positive achievements, and remains one of the most complicated, if not the most complicated, bilateral relationship we have in the world.[22]

The formalities of this rapport had been worked out by the Council on Foreign Relations (CFR), the foreign policy think tank of political and business interests, since the early

---

21 Chang and Halliday, *Mao*, 601.
22 Richard Holbrooke, Asia Society Gala 50th anniversary dinner speeches, http://www.asiasociety.org/support/specialevents/anniversary_dinner/galaspeeches.html.

1960s. Peter Grosse writes in his CFR-sanctioned history of that institution:

> The Council turned in earnest to the problem of communist China early in the 1960s. Various Council publications had started developing the idea of a 'two-China' policy—recognition of both the Nationalist government of Taiwan and the communist government on the mainland. This, Council authors suggested, might be the least bad policy direction. Professor A. Doak Barnett published a trail-blazing book for the Council in 1960, *Communist China and Asia*. A major Council study of relations between the United States and China commenced in 1964, the year China exploded its first nuclear bomb; the group met systematically for the next four years. 'Contentment with the present stalemate in relations with the Chinese is not statesmanship,' declared Robert Blum of the Asia Society, the first director of the project. 'American impatience and the strong currents of political emotion often make it impossible to plan ahead to manage our policy in a persevering but flexible way.'[23]

Hence, the CFR was formulating a policy for the dumping of Taiwan and the recognition of Mao's China in a typically Machiavellian manner that would make it appear as though the US was not dumping Taiwan, while simultaneously ensuring that China would come into the 'world community.' Grosse continues:

> In 1969 the Council summed up the project under the title, *The United States and China in World Affairs*, [*sic*] publication came just as Richard Nixon, a longtime

---

23 Peter Grosse, *Continuing the Inquiry: The Council on Foreign Relations from 1921 to 1996* (New York: Council on Foreign Relations, 2006). '"X" Leads the Way.' The entire book, which frankly describes the history and influence of the CFR, can be read online at: Council on Foreign Relations: http://www.cfr.org/about/history/cfr/index.html.

and outspoken foe of Chinese communism, became president of the United States. (Some months earlier, Nixon himself had chosen *Foreign Affairs* as his forum for exploring a fresh look at Asia in general, and China in particular.) Tilting at the long-prevailing freeze, the Council's project defined a two-China policy with careful analysis. It advocated acquiescence in mainland Chinese membership in the United Nations, and argued that America must 'abandon its effort to maintain the fiction that the Nationalist regime is the government of China.'[24]

Grosse concluded by proudly citing Kissinger and Cyrus Vance as CFR members in their pivotal roles in inaugurating a process that has made China a world power:

Kissinger, acting as Nixon's national security adviser, embarked on a secret mission to Beijing in 1971,[25] to make official, exploratory contact with the communist regime. Nixon himself followed in 1972. The delicate process of normalizing diplomatic relations between the United States and China was completed in 1978 by Kissinger's successor as secretary of state, Cyrus R. Vance, a leading Council officer before and after his government service.[26]

Kissinger made his first trip to China in 1972 to plan a visit from Nixon. The Americans offered as a preliminary goodwill gesture the abandonment of Taiwan and official recognition of Red China, and offered to get China into the United Nations, as per the CFR blueprint. Additionally, the US would provide China with information on all its

---

24 Ibid., 43.

25 Grosse mentions in a note that: 'Accompanying Kissinger on this momentous flight was his personal aide, Winston Lord, a former Foreign Service officer. Lord . . . became president of the Council on Foreign Relations in 1977 . . .'

26 Ibid., 43–44.

dealings with Russia. Kissinger also told the Chinese that the US would be withdrawing from South Vietnam,[27] and that American troops would soon be pulled out of South Korea. China was not asked for any concessions.[28]

In 1973, Kissinger assured Mao that the US would come to China's assistance if attacked by Russia.[29] The groundwork was also laid for the technological and industrial build up of China, and therefore the establishment of the military strength that Mao had failed to achieve via the USSR. On 6 July, Kissinger told Mao's envoy:

> I have talked to the French Foreign Minister about our interest in strengthening the PRC [People's Republic of China]. We will do what we can to encourage our allies to speed up requests they receive from you on items for Chinese defense.

> In particular you have asked for some Rolls-Royce [engine] technology. Under existing regulations we have to oppose this, but we have worked out a procedure with the British where they will go ahead anyway. *We will take a formal position in opposition, but only that. Don't be confused by what we do publicly . . .*[30]

Kissinger's last sentence is a key to understanding world history and politics: '*Don't be confused by what we do publicly.*' It is the manner in which high politics works behind the scenes, and has little to do with what is given out to the news media for public consumption.

In 1973, David Rockefeller went to China and waxed lyrical about the Mao regime, writing: 'The social experiment

---

27   However, a united Vietnam within the Soviet orbit was not in China's interests.
28   Chang and Halliday, *Mao*, 604–5.
29   Ibid., 612.
30   Ibid., 612–13. Emphasis added.

in China under Chairman Mao's leadership is one of the most important and successful in human history . . .'[31] David Rockefeller's Standard Oil obtained exclusive rights to China's oil exploration; his Chase Manhattan Bank to industrial finance.

The US-China relationship developed under the auspices of Rockefeller's Trilateral Commission think tankers, such as National Security Adviser Zbigniew Brzezinski, who dominated the Carter regime from the president down, when in 1978 the 'normalization of relations' with China was finalised. When Taiwan was dumped in 1978 and diplomatic relations were formally established with the PRC, Leonard Woodcock, an early member of the Trilateral Commission, became the first US Ambassador to China. Apart from the Rockefeller interests, other early globalist corporations whose chief executives were Trilateralists included: Coca-Cola, given the soft drink monopoly (J. Paul Austin, a backer of Carter), Boeing Aircraft (T. A. Wilson), and Mitsui Petrochemical (Yoshizo Ikeda). Japanese Trilateralists were heavily involved with early dealings in China. Mitsubishi, whose chairman Chujiro Funjino was chairman of the Japanese Trilateral Commission Executive Committee, got the contract to modernise the Shanghai shipyards, the largest in China. Hitachi Ltd. (president Hirokichi Yoshiyama) got a $100,000,000 contract to supply equipment for the Paoshan steelworks and to expand the Hungchi Shipyards. Nippon Steel (Yoshihiro Inayama) was involved with constructing a giant steel plant near Shanghai.[32]

The most compelling reason that confrontation between the US and China is unlikely is that the economies of the two are symbiotic, which cannot be said in regard to the

---

31 David Rockefeller, 'From a China Traveller,' *New York Times*, 10 August 1973.

32 Antony Sutton, *Trilaterals Over Washington* (Arizona: The August Corp., 1978), vol. 2, chapter 6.

relationship between China and Russia, or Russia and the US. Dr. Niall Ferguson stated: 'Since April 2002 the central banks of China and Hong Kong have bought 96 billion dollars of US government securities.' This means that 'the US is reliant on the central bank of the People's Republic of China for the financing of about 4% per year of its federal borrowing.' Ferguson refers to the 'growing interdependence' between the economies of the US and China: 'Far from being strategic rivals, these two empires have the air of economic partners. The only question is which of the two is the more dependent, which, to be precise, stands to lose more in the event of a crisis in their amicable relationship, now over thirty years old. . . .'[33] Ferguson also states: 'Many commentators have noted the very muted, even quiescent reaction of China to recent American interventions. Fewer have appreciated the extent to which China now helps underwrite American power.'[34]

In contrast, the relations between Russia and the US, with increasing US provocations in regard to Russia's neighbours of the former Soviet bloc, have set the US and Russia on course towards another cold war.

Continuing the Rockefeller-China legacy is the apparently enigmatic Nicholas Rockefeller whose very existence has even been questioned.[35] A profile of Nicholas Rockefeller

---

33 Niall Ferguson, *Colossus: The Rise and Fall of the American Empire* (London: Allen Lane, 2004), 261.

34 Ibid., 262.

35 'Enigmatic' because there has been doubt expressed by 'sceptics' as to whether he actually exists, putting his existence down to the invention of 'conspiracy theorists.' The question can quite readily be answered by referring to his influential involvement with the RAND Corporation and the CFR: He is a member of the Council on Foreign Relations, the International Institute of Strategic Studies, the Advisory Board of RAND, the Corporate Advisory Board of the Pacific Council on International Relations, the Board of the Western Justice Center Foundation, and the Central China Development Council and has served as a participant in the World Economic Forum and the Aspen Institute. He also serves as a director of the Pacific Rim Cultural Foundation, and is a member of the board of visitors of the law schools of the University of Oregon and of Pepperdine University. http://

states of his China connections:

> Nicholas' China practice includes transactions with China's largest banks, energy companies, communications entities and real estate enterprises as well as with China's principal cities and leading provinces. He was chosen as a board member of the Central China Construction and Development Commission and as a director of the Xiwai International School of Shanghai International University. He has appeared numerous times on CCTV and other China media.[36]

There is also doubt that Nicholas Rockefeller co-authored a book[37] with banker Patrick DeSouza, Rockefeller's name not appearing as the co-author, thereby again suggesting that Nicholas Rockefeller is a myth. However, the fact is that DeSouza edited the book that is a collection of essays by members of the CFR. DeSouza has served on the National Security Council under President Clinton and is a Fellow of the CFR. As for Nicholas Rockefeller and the DeSouza book, Nicholas wrote Chapter 19, 'Middle Market Capitalism in China,' pp. 347–56. The book moreover is described as 'A Council on Foreign Relations Book.' Nicholas Rockefeller was one of the CFR members selected to contribute to this important CFR compendium. Far from being mythical, Nicholas is a major US player in China and an influential figure in foreign policy think tanks.

In addition to the Rockefellers, the Soros financial and NGO world network has become an important factor in the globalist power structure. Soros, like the Rockefellers, is a pro-China enthusiast and seeks the incorporation of China into a 'new world order,' with China playing a leading role.

---

www.nicholasrockefeller.net/

36   http://www.nicholasrockefeller.net/
37   Patrick J. DeSouza, ed., *Economic Strategy and National Security: A Next Generation Approach* (Boulder, CO: Westview Press, 2000).

A report of an interview by Soros with the London *Financial Times* in 2009 states:

> Billionaire globalist George Soros told the *Financial Times* during an interview that China will supplant the United States as the leader of the new world order and that America should not resist the country's decline as the dollar weakens, living standards drop, and a new global currency is introduced.
>
> Asked what Obama should discuss when he visits China next month, Soros stated, 'This would be the time because I think you really need to bring China into the creation of a new world order, financial world order,' adding that China was a reluctant member of the IMF who didn't make enough of a contribution.
>
> 'I think you need a new world order that China has to be part of the process of creating it and they have to buy in, they have to own it in the same way as the United States owns . . . the current order,' said Soros, adding that the G20 was a move in this direction . . .
>
> Soros said the world would have to go through a 'painful adjustment' following the decline of the dollar and the introduction of a global currency. Reading between the lines, he essentially threatened to kill the dollar completely if the United States did not get on board with the global currency.
>
> Soros predicted that China would become the new engine of the global economy, replacing the U.S., and that this would slow economic growth and reduce living standards. Soros characterized the United States as a drag on the global economy because of the declining dollar.[38]

---

38   Paul Joseph Watson, 'Soros: China Will Lead New World Order. Billionaire

The following month *Forbes* reported that, 'George Soros is pouring money into Chinese stocks. That's because the billionaire believes China will emerge as the big winner after the global financial crisis passes, while the United States will lose the most in the long run from the recent turmoil. . . .' Soros is keen to invest in China. To understand more about China's latest social and economic developments—and to help him spot out investment targets—he recently met some Chinese scholars and experts in Budapest, where he was born in 1930. China is likely to be a 'positive force' in the global economy, Soros said, while the United States will be 'limping along.'[39]

The globalist faction based around Soros and Rockefeller interests has no motive in promoting 'regime change' in China or any geopolitical shift that would destabilise China. It is Russia that does not fit into the 'new world order,' and the natural bulwark against Russia is China, as in the days of the Cold War. More recently, Soros reiterated the rise of China as the up-and-coming factor in the 'new world order,' stating: 'China has risen very rapidly by looking out for its own interests. They have now got to accept responsibility for world order and the interests of other people as well.'[40] Therefore, according to Soros, there needs to be a shift in attitude among Western states that will encourage China to play its full, even dominant, part in a new international system.

Foreign Policy[41] editorialised that:

Globalist Warns Americans Against Resisting New Global Financial System,' *Prison Planet.com*, 28 October 2009, http://www.prisonplanet.com/soros-china-will-lead-new-world-order.html.

39 Vivian Kwok and Robert Olsen, 'Soros Turns to China,' *Forbes*, 13 November 2009, http://www.forbes.com/2009/11/13/soros-china-investments-markets-equity-billionaire.html.

40 Joshua Keating, 'Soros: China Has Better Functioning Government Than US,' *Foreign Policy*, 16 November 2010.

41 Not to be confused with *Foreign Policy Journal*.

Mr Soros even went so far as to say that at times China wields more power than the U.S. because of the political gridlock in Washington. 'Today China has not only a more vigorous economy, but actually a better functioning government than the United States,' he said, a hard statement for him to make because he spent much of his life donating to anti-communist groups in Eastern Europe.[42]

What *Foreign Policy* editorial writers are unlikely to understand is that it is not 'communism' *per se* to which Soros and other luminaries of international capital are opposed, but those types of 'communism' that do not accommodate their designs, while other types of communism, such as the Chinese, are not only acceptable but beneficial; just as international capital will support or oppose, according to pragmatic or dialectical interests, democracy and dictatorship, 'Left' and 'Right.' Any desired change in China will be hoped for in a less dramatic manner than the 'regime change' that has been brought about across the world by the 'colour revolutions' that George Soros and his 'Open Society' network, and US NGOs such as the National Endowment for Democracy and USAID, have instigated, firstly in the former Soviet bloc states and most lately with the so-called 'Arab Spring' that is still being fermented as this is written.[43] A 'return to authoritarianism' and the 'wrong direction'—as the globalists are terming it—maintained by Russia under Putin are the primary threats to this globalist paradigm. The US sees Russia as a potential threat to what the Russians call its 'world hegemony.' As noted previously, China is willing to see the US share its sphere of influence in Central Asia, whereas the Russians are adverse. Even now, without any real strategic threat, the US challenges Russia by deploying missiles directed towards the Russian frontier, in Russia's former spheres of influence in Eastern

42 Keating, 'Soros.'

43 See: K. R. Bolton, *Revolution from Above* (London: Arktos Media, 2011), 213–44.

Europe. Poland and the Czech Republic became members of NATO in 1999. In 2008 Russia stated that US plans to deploy missiles and radar systems in the two former Warsaw Pact states is a threat to Russian security.[44] Strategically, Russia must perceive herself as being encircled by the US and China in previous Russian spheres; the US with its missile deployment in Eastern Europe, and China with its alliance with Mongolia.

When in 2006 the US labour organisation AFL-CIO petitioned the Bush Administration to place economic restrictions on China in regard to China's labour laws, this was directly opposed by a united front of big business associations. Their letter to President Bush is instructive in regard to the continuing pro-China attitude prevalent among influential business identities. Among the 14 signatories were the Business Round Table, the Emergency Committee for American Trade, the National Foreign Trade Council, the US Council for International Business, the US Chamber of Commerce, and the US-China Business Council.[45] They called on Bush to reject the AFL-CIO petition to the Office of the US Trade Representative. The attitude of one of their number, Thomas J. Donohue, CEO of the US Chamber of Commerce, was stated before a 2004 conference of the Asia Society: 'The China genie is out of the bottle, and there's no putting him back—nor would we want to even if we could.'[46]

THE US AND CHINA'S MILITARY BUILD-UP

It is naïve to think that the US will act decisively against China when the two powers exist in economic symbiosis and do not have significant geopolitical conflicts of interest

---

44 'Russia Says U.S. Missile Shield Will Harm European Security,' RIA Novosti, Moscow, 15 July 2008, http://en.rian.ru/russia/20080715/114016639.html.

45 Dated 23 June 2006.

46 http://www.asiasociety.org/speeches/donohue04.html

that will necessitate American military intervention. Rather, despite the occasional American posturing on the world stage about 'human rights' in China, the US has not used this against China in the manner by which it is used to subvert and overthrow states that are a genuine annoyance to the US, as per the contrived 'Arab Spring,' and the noises that are made against states marked for 'regime change' such as Myanmar, Syria, Iran, and Venezuela, or, most significantly, the campaign against Russia for being insufficiently 'democratic,' and taking a 'wrong turn.'[47]

Not only has the US failed to act in any decisive manner against its supposed rival, but Sino-American military cooperation is of long duration. Given the Sino-American economic symbiosis, a military alliance, under some pretext such as the 'war on terrorism,' a catchphrase used to rationalise a multiplicity of US global ambitions, is a natural development. While there are important critics of US relations with China, they are not the only wire-pullers in Washington, or the dominant faction, and plutocratic interests such as those centred around Goldman Sachs, the Rockefellers, and Soros, et al., are Sinophiles. A report by the Congressional Research Service prepared for 'members and committees of Congress,' outlines the historical relations between the US and China since the Cold War, when the states were in accord vis-à-vis the USSR. This relationship laid the basis for ongoing Sino-American cooperation in terms of 'strategic dialogue, reciprocal exchanges in functional areas, and arms sales.'

In 1984, US policymakers worked to advance discussions on military technological cooperation with China. There were commercial sales to the People's Liberation Army that included Sikorsky Aircraft's sale of twenty-four S-70C

---

47   Jack Kemp et al., *Russia's Wrong Direction: What the United States Can and Should Do*, Independent Task Force Report no. 57 (New York: Council on Foreign Relations, 2006), http://www.cfr.org/publication/9997/.

transport helicopters (an unarmed version of the Black Hawk helicopter) and General Electric's sale of five gas turbine engines for two naval destroyers. Between 1985 and 1987, the United States also agreed to four programs of government-to-government Foreign Military Sales (FMS): modernisation of artillery ammunition production facilities; modernisation of avionics in F-8 fighters; sale of four Mark-46 antisubmarine torpedoes; and sale of four AN/TPQ-37 artillery-locating radars.[48]

From 1989 to 1993 there was a disruption of military and trade relations between the two as the US's response to the Tiananmen Square massacre.[49] Repressions of this type in almost any other state would have resulted in major consequences, including calls for 'regime change' and the fomenting of a 'coloured revolution,' but the relationship between the two was quickly resumed, with some sporadic fluctuations during the 1990s and since. In 2001, the Bush Administration expanded cooperation, including Pentagon 'mil-to-mil' (military to military) exchanges.[50] Another hiccup occurred when there was a collision of US and Chinese aircraft over the South China Sea in 2001, but top level military consultation and exchanges were soon back on track.[51] In other words, while the road has had a few rocks in the way, and perhaps even nothing more than staged shadow-boxing as in the Cold War, for public consumption, it is nonetheless a forward movement. From 2007 to 2010,[52] China acted in a provocative manner towards the US, perhaps on the basis that shadow-boxing looks good on the world stage and any low level actions in regard to the US will not result in any significant consequences. During

48 Shirley A. Kan, 'U.S.-China Military Contacts: Issues for Congress,' Congressional Research Service, 19 June 2012, 1, http://www.fas.org/sgp/crs/natsec/RL32496.pdf.
49 Ibid., 2.
50 Ibid.
51 Ibid.
52 Ibid., 4.

the same period, Sino-American cooperation and dialogue in regional and international forums and dealing with piracy continued unchanged. The shadow-boxing serves US interests in the region well enough, since, as in the Cold War era and the 'Russian menace,' the US can maintain its big brother persona throughout the Pacific region while not undertaking anything that will seriously challenge China's interests.

In 1994, the US-China Joint Defense Conversion Commission (JDCC) was established 'to facilitate economic cooperation and technical exchanges and cooperation in the area of defence conversion, but this had to be terminated due to pressure from Congress.'[53] This indicates that the US administration must tread a path of caution in dealing with China in cognisance of domestic pressure, but that at the highest echelons of US administrations a quite different policy is advocated. It seems, however, that cooperation has been taking place in a manner that is planned to bypass public concerns:

> In early 1999, under the Clinton Administration, the *Washington Times* disclosed the existence of a 'Gameplan for 1999 U.S.-Sino Defense Exchanges,' and Pentagon spokesperson Kenneth Bacon confirmed that an exchange program had been under way for years. Representative Dana Rohrabacher wrote a letter to Secretary of Defense William Cohen, saying that 'after reviewing the "Game Plan," it appears evident that a number of events involving PLA logistics, acquisitions, quartermaster and chemical corps representatives may benefit PLA modernization to the detriment of our allies in the Pacific region and, ultimately, the lives of own service members.' He requested a detailed written description of various exchanges.[54]

---

53   Ibid., 11.
54   Ibid., 12.

The bypassing of US laws by the Clinton Administration continued under Bush.[55] In the Defense Department's 2008 report to Congress, Deputy Secretary of Defense Gordon England defined one of the primary aims of US China policy as being to 'encourage China to play a constructive and peaceful role in the Asia-Pacific region; to act as a partner in addressing common security challenges; and to emerge as a responsible stakeholder in the world.'[56] While this might be regarded as well-meaning diplomacy to assure world peace, at face value it is America's statement of intent that China should become a US partner, an attitude that is far from US intentions towards Russia. It is a statement in accord with the advice of veteran foreign policy globalists such as Kissinger and Brzezinski, and plutocrats such as David Rockefeller and George Soros, who see China in partnership with the US and primarily against Russia, as in the Cold War era.[57] The common objectives of the US and China in the Brave New World have recently been clarified:

Secretary of State Hillary Clinton gave a speech on 10 April 2012, stressing that 'China is not the Soviet Union,' 'we are not on the brink of a new Cold War in Asia,' and that 'this is not 1912 when friction between a declining Britain and a rising Germany set the stage for global conflict.' Apparently responding positively to Clinton, on 3 May in Beijing, China's leader Hu Jintao called for a 'new type of great power relationship' that is reassuring to both countries and to others. Hu promptly dispatched General Liang Guanglie as the Defense Minister to visit the United States on 4–10 May, where he echoed Hu by saying that 'China and the United States should build a new type of state-to-state relationship that is not in the

55   Ibid.
56   Ibid., 18.
57   Kenneth Rapoza, 'Kissinger: US-China Not Competing for World Domination,' *Forbes*, 28 June 2011, http://www.forbes.com/sites/kenrapoza/2011/06/28/kissinger-us-china-not-competing-for-world-domination/.

stereotype that the two major powers are predestined to engage into confrontation or conflict.' The PLA supports a positive tone for US-PRC ties.[58]

THE SACRIFICE OF TIBET

The tragedy of Tibet's subjugation to China is reflective of the way Western business and China work in accord for the mutual exploitation of a country's resources. It is an example of why the US will not conflict with China on such issues. It is also an example of the duplicitous manner by which US foreign policy operates.

While it is being claimed that there has been a long association between the Dalai Lama and his supporters and the CIA,[59] as is generally the case such a relationship has been duplicitous. In a scenario that seems to be analogous to the CIA relationship with anti-Castro Cubans[60] leading up to the 'Bay of Pigs' fiasco, and indeed the manner by which the US betrayed Chiang Kai-shek to the Maoists,[61] the CIA backed the Tibetan resistance in the early years of China's occupation for what seems to have been the purpose of sabotage. From 1958 the CIA began training Tibetans in Virginia and Colorado's Rocky Mountains, where 259 Tibetans were trained in Camp Hale over the next five years. Lhamo Tsering, a senior resistance leader and the CIA's chief coordinator, documented this fateful saga with the Tibetans, which was the subject of a BBC documentary produced by his son, Tenzing Sonam, and the latter's wife, Ritu Sarin.

58 Kan, op. cit., 30–31.

59 For example: 'The Dalai Lama and the CIA,' a typically superficial Maoist analysis from *Revolutionary Worker*, no. 765, 17 July 1994, http://revcom.us/a/firstvol/tibet/cia5.htm.

60 Mario Lazo, *Dagger in the Heart: American Policy Failures in Cuba* (New York: Twin Circle Publishing Co., 1968).

61 Chang and Halliday, *Mao*, 304–11.

In a review of the BBC documentary *The Shadow Circus: The CIA in Tibet*, Ramananda Sengupta cites some of those involved as stating:

'We had great expectations when we went to America. We thought perhaps they would even give us an atom bomb to take back,' says Tenzin Tsultrim. 'In the training period, we learned that the objective was to gain our independence,' adds another grizzled veteran. But the Americans had other ideas. 'The whole idea was to keep the Chinese occupied, keep them annoyed, keep them disturbed. Nobody wanted to go to war over Tibet . . . It was a nuisance operation. Basically, nothing more,' says former CIA agent Sam Halpern.[62]

In 1959, following a revolt, where Tibetans held control over large areas of the south, the CIA assisted with the Dalai Lama's entry into India when his arrest by the Chinese seemed likely. There followed a mass exodus, leaving few resistance fighters.

Undeterred, the CIA parachuted four groups of Camp Hale trainees inside Tibet between 1959 and 1960 to contact the remaining resistance groups. But the missions resulted in the massacre of all but a few of the team members.[63] A familiar scenario for anti-communists backed by the US and/or CIA follows:

The CIA cooked up a fresh operation in Mustang, a remote corner of Nepal that juts into Tibet. Nearly two thousand Tibetans gathered there to continue their fight for freedom. A year later, the CIA made its first arms drop in Mustang. Organised on the lines of a modern army, the guerrillas were led by Bapa Yeshe, a former monk.

---

62   R. Sengupta, 'The CIA Circus: Tibet's Forgotten Army,' Friends of Tibet (India), 15 February 1999, http://www.friendsoftibet.org/databank/usdefence/usd7.html.

63   Ibid.

'As soon as we received the aid, the Americans started scolding us like children. They said that we had to go into Tibet immediately. Sometimes I wished they hadn't sent us the arms at all,' says Yeshe.

The Mustang guerrillas conducted cross-border raids into Tibet. The CIA made two more arms drops to the Mustang force, the last in May 1965. Then, in early 1969, the agency abruptly cut off all support.[64] The CIA explained that one of the main conditions the Chinese had set for establishing diplomatic relations with the US was to stop all connections and all assistance to the Tibetans. Says Roger McCarthy, an ex-CIA man, 'It still smarts that we pulled out in the manner we did.'

Thinley Paljor, a surviving resistance fighter, was among the thousands shattered by this volte-face. 'We felt deceived, we felt our usefulness to the CIA is finished. They were only thinking short-term for their own personal gain, not for the long-term interests of the Tibetan people.'

In 1974, arm-twisted by the Chinese, the Nepalese government sent troops to Mustang to demand the surrender of the guerrillas. Fearing a bloody confrontation, the Dalai Lama sent the resistance fighters a taped message, asking them to surrender. They did so, reluctantly. Some committed suicide soon afterwards. . . .

'The film is for the younger Tibetans, who are unaware of the resistance, as well as for Americans, who don't know how their own government used and betrayed the

---

64 The 'abrupt cutting off' of arms supplies in such circumstances seems to be a constant of US policy. Chiang in China, and Somoza in Nicaragua were dealt deathblows in similar situations. For the latter's predicament see: Anastasio Somoza and Jack Cox, *Nicaragua Betrayed* (Boston: Western Island Publishers, 1980).

resistance,' says Tenzing. 'Though it was a story begging to be told, funding it was almost impossible,' adds Ritu.[65]

Hence, if certain American-based interests can be seen as being involved in certain pro-Tibet lobbies, this does not mean that one can expect there to be a consistent and effective pro-Tibet policy from the US, nor that global capital is in accord with a position toward China vis-à-vis Tibet. More likely, any such feigned friendship emanating from the US will be duplicitous.

Soros interests in Tibet are not the same as the actions of his network towards a myriad of other states that have suffered his 'colour revolutions.' For example, Soros' daughter Andrea established the Trace Foundation in 1993 to work in the Tibetan Plateau, after having taught as an English teacher in the region. The Trace Foundation clearly works with the Chinese authorities, and would not last long if it did not. While there is every reason to believe that this humanitarian effort is designed to encourage economic development in Tibet according to the Soros agenda of the 'open society'[66] this does not appear to equate with Soros' agenda in other states where he has been responsible for 'regime change,' often accompanied by violence. The Trace Foundation would more likely be a means of partnership rather than that of subversion. It can be argued that a 'colour revolution' in China or in Tibet is impossible, nonetheless are there tangible reasons as to why global capital would actually desire 'regime change' in either place when investments are protected by draconian measures.

As is known the Rockefellers and Soros, Goldman Sachs, and others have intimate business connections with China. Soros and the Rockefellers believe that China can

---

65 Sengupta, op. cit.
66 Andrea Soros, 'President's Message,' Trace Foundation, http://www.trace.org/about/about.html.

be integrated within the world economic system without the need for 'regime change.' Indeed, such change would undoubtedly cause wholesale disruption from which China, like the fiasco of American intervention in Iraq, might never recover, and in the instance of China particularly, the world economic system being cultivated by such globalist interests would stand in danger of irredeemable collapse. Soros' own attitudes toward China is in accord with that of the Rockefellers, as cited previously.

Clearly, Soros and other globalist interests have no interest in undermining the stability of China, nor in freeing Tibet from Chinese control. Certainly from the viewpoint of Soros, the Rockefellers, et al., China does indeed need to be more 'open,' and this is indeed inexorably taking place. While the investment and opportunities of international capital in China are well known enough or easy enough to discover, not so obvious is the position in regard to Tibet, and why the elimination of Chinese authority over Tibet would not serve the interests of global capital.

Tibet is China's tenth Special Economic Zone.[67] This means that the Tibetan Autonomous Region has been granted 'special' status in being opened up to foreign capital for exploitation in partnership with the Chinese administration. China ensures order and stability and Western-style economic development in Tibet. It does not seem plausible that Western-based business interests would want that situation to change in favour of one that returns Tibet to a feudal state. Such regimes are seen as outmoded hindrances to maximum profits by international capital, unable or unwilling to fit into a world economic system. A sovereign, traditional Tibet is precisely the type of regime that Soros, the National Endowment for Democracy, and a vast array of other NGOs have sought to depose in the

---

67   'China's Economic Zones and STIPS,' www.chinaculture.org/library/2008-02/07/
     content_69814_3.htm.

post-Soviet bloc states, attempting to halt any shift towards tradition. Recently, the Duma has sought to limit the subversive activities of NGOs in Russia and oblige them to register as 'foreign agents,' as these organisations, as in other states, back the political opposition and are therefore active in interfering in domestic politics.

Tibet is richly endowed with mineral resources. While Serbia was a target of NATO because of the mineral wealth of Kosovo,[68] the present regime in Tibet is ideal for the exploitation of the region by Big Business.

A recent announcement to 'leapfrog' Tibet's economic development was announced by the Chinese, veiled as being in the interests of the Tibetan people:

> 'Rational and orderly exploitation of Tibet's mineral resources will power the region's "leapfrog development,"' said Dorje (many Tibetans go by a single name). The Communist Party of China (CPC) Central Committee announced plans to achieve 'leapfrog development' in Tibet at the fifth meeting on the work of Tibet in January, including building the region into a 'strategic reserve of natural resources' with an aim to reduce poverty among the Tibetan people.

> Over the last eight years, Tibet has witnessed over 12 percent economic growth annually as 180 billion yuan ($26 billion) was poured into infrastructure in the region, mostly by the central government, he said.

> The central government would continue to pour investment into Tibet in an effort to develop the economy of the remote, impoverished region and raise

---

68 That is, the Trepa mining complex, which has the richest lead, lignite and zinc mines in Europe. Sara Flounders, 'Kosovo: "The War Is About the Mines,"' 30 July 1998, http://www.iacenter.org/folder04/kosovo_mines.htm.

the living standards of its people, said Zhang Qingli, the region's Communist Party secretary.

Tibet has more than 3,000 proven mineral reserves containing 102 varieties of resources. It has China's biggest proven chromium and copper reserves, according to figures from the regional land and resources department. . . .

'But Tibet's mineral industry is still fledgling, contributing about 3 percent to the local economy,' Dorje told Xinhua.

. . . Tibet has marked nine special zones for mineral industries, including a special economic zone centred on the Yulong Copper Mine, one of China's biggest copper mines in the eastern Qamdo Prefecture, and a salt lake area in the northwest that is expected to become a major base for saline minerals and lithium. . . .[69]

While the monopoly capitalism of yesteryear relied on the weapons and administrations of the old European empires under which they exploited the resources of colonies until capital truly globalised and the empires became too restrictive, today international capital has the military and administrative structures of the US and in this instance of China. It is unlikely to be a situation that international capital wants changing for the sake of Tibetan freedom and civilisation, while China is providing the infrastructure, administration and policing.

The following extracts from a submission to the United Nations by a consultative NGO are instructive in regard to the capitalist-Chinese axis exploiting Tibet:

---

69   'Tibet to Step Up Exploitation of Mineral Resources,' *China Daily*, 13 March 2010, http://www.chinadaily.com.cn/china/2010-03/13/content_9584983.htm.

2. The People's Republic of China's (PRC) policy and practice of population transfer into Tibet, in aid of its efforts to develop Tibet economically and exploit its resources, has been well-documented. In June 1999, President Jiang Zemin announced the PRC's 'Western Development' campaign. In theory, this refers to a policy of developing western China by improving its economic infrastructure and providing more funds for education, the environment and technological development. In practice, it represents a systematic escalation of the long-standing policy of exploiting natural resources in Tibet and Xinjiang for export to China. In aid of its exploitation of Tibet, the PRC has received, and is seeking, the assistance of transnational corporations.

3. With the support of international corporations, mining operations in Tibet threaten to violate the Tibetans' right to self-determination; that is, their right to freely determine their economic, social and cultural development. For example, Australian-owned Sino Mining International (SMI) and other foreign investors plan to develop the Tanjiashan gold deposit in northern Tibet. Tibetans, however, are not participating in the decisions to exploit their natural resources. They will not enjoy the economic benefits these activities bring, as the resources are mined for export. Moreover, evidence indicates that such projects are pursued in an environmentally destructive manner, polluting Tibet's lands, forests and waters. Tibetan communities will bear the long-term social and environmental costs of destructive mining practices.

4. Significant reserves of oil, gas and hydropower are also located in Xinjiang and Qinghai (Tibetan: Amdo) Provinces. China's oil and gas reserves already have lured foreign investment. BP Amoco invested $578 million in the Chinese oil company, PetroChina, to help complete

the 'Sebei-Lanzhou' pipeline, which now runs 2500 km from Tibet's Tsaidam Basin to Lanzhou. Italian ENI/ Agip also assisted in the construction of this pipeline across the Tibetan plateau. This internationally-financed energy project was developed without consulting Tibetans, without providing any compensation to the Tibetans for their natural resources, and without assessing its dramatic environmental and social impact.

5. China's plan to construct a 4000 km oil pipeline from Xinjiang to Shanghai, known as the 'West-East Pipeline' project, similarly exploits the people's resources without their participation or benefit. This pipeline will eventually connect with the Sebei-Lanzhou pipeline. To finance this estimated $18 billion project, the PRC is entering into partnerships with Shell, Exxon/Mobil and other transnational corporations. Without their financial backing, the PRC simply could not guarantee the success of this unprecedented project. According to *Business Week*, because China views this project as the backbone of its national energy plan and a springboard for future foreign investments, China initially has been willing to pay lip service to examining the project's social and environmental impacts. Nevertheless, the construction of this pipeline raises grave concerns about the importation of Chinese laborers to work on the pipeline, long-term environmental degradation, lack of compensation to Tibetans and Uighurs for their land, and long-term economic control over the region.

6. Virtually all of the natural resources and material wealth extracted from Tibet are channelled back to enrich China's eastern regions. The proposed Qinghai-Tibet railway will also serve to accelerate the extraction of minerals and other natural resources, as well as promote the 'assimilation of Tibet into the motherland' by increasing Chinese migration. The purpose of such large-scale infrastructure

projects, according to Tibet Information Network, is to facilitate the extraction of raw materials and goods out of Tibet and into the wealthier, more industrialized eastern Chinese regions. *The People's Daily* acknowledged that this project will bring an 'unprecedented mammoth transfer of resources.' . . .

7. Another example of transnational corporations participating in violations of the Tibetans' rights to self-determination, to religious and cultural freedom, and to a protected environment, is the Yamdrok Tso hydroelectric project. This project was built over the strong objections of many Tibetans (some of whom were jailed for objecting) as it threatens the environment surrounding a lake considered sacred by the Tibetan people. Without substantial participation by transnational corporations, which supplied equipment and expertise, this project could not have been built. Moreover, the primary purpose of the project is to supply additional electric power to the Lhasa area in order to support the transfer of more Chinese settlers into this region.[1]

In 2003 the official Chinese media reported on the growth of foreign investment in Tibet:

Improving investment environment has attracted increasing overseas capital to the Tibet Autonomous Region in southwest China, an official said in Lhasa, Tibet on Sep. 16.

Tibet has approved 14 joint ventures with contractual overseas investment amounting to 4.31 million US dollars since 2001, with 2.16 million US dollars of

---

1 'Transnational Corporations and Human Rights,' International League for Human Rights, 3 July 2002, Tibet Justice Center, http://www.tibetjustice.org/ reports/un/unint10.html.

it already materialized, said Dopuje, deputy head of the investment promotion bureau with the regional development and reform commission. . . .

Dopuje attributed the growing overseas investment to China's campaign to open up the vast western regions and a range of preferential policies Tibet has introduced for investors.

The regional government revoked more than 60 articles of regulations that restricted economic development, and improved the investment environment by simplifying approval procedures in 2001, said the official.[2]

A 2008 report cited the enormous increase in foreign investment into Tibet, particularly in regard to mineral prospecting:

LHASA—Lhasa, the capital of west China's Tibet Autonomous Region, received 455.5 million US dollars of overseas investment in the first seven months of 2008, up 33 percent year-on-year.

The majority of the investment, or 95.3 percent of the total, went into the industrial sector, which includes non-ferrous metal smelting, the manufacturing of machinery and chemical products, food processing and geological prospecting, according to figures from the city's statistics bureau on Monday . . .[3]

In 2010 China initiated a further programme to encourage investment, stating that, 'It was known that the foreign-

2   'Overseas Investment in Tibet Increasing,' Consulate General of the People's Republic of China in San Francisco, 24 December 2003, http://www. chinaconsulatesf.org/eng/zhuanti/xz/t56913.htm.

3   'Tibet Reports Double-Digit Growth in Overseas Investment,' *China Daily*, 19 August 2008, http://www.chinadaily.com.cn/china/2008-08/19/content_6951483. htm.

invested enterprises approved by governmental sectors shall enjoy related preferential polices of the state and the autonomous region.'[4]

The Chinese regime over Tibet represents the ideal capitalist scenario: a police state protecting and encouraging foreign investment. Why would the business coteries that are generally in control of the US want this situation to change? Any statement to the contrary is likely to be meaningless rhetoric.

As the following chapter shows, China's control of the headwaters located in Tibet is one of the most crucial—indeed, life and death—issues for a vast expanse of people.

4   'Tibet Guides Foreign Investment to Characteristic and Dominant Industries,' *Invest in China*, 13 April 2010, http://fdi.gov.cn/pub/FDI_EN/News/ Investmentupdates/t20100413_120314.htm.

Scenarios for Crises

Rivalry over Water Resources as a Potential Cause of Conflict in Asia

Rival: 'From L. *rivalis* "a rival"; originally, "one who uses the same stream" (or "one on the opposite side of the stream"), from *rivus* "brook."'[5]

Just how apt the Latin etymology of the English words 'rival' and 'rivalry' are as having derived from one's relationship with water might soon be seen in conflicts over water resources that will be particularly acute in the Indo-Pacific region. While much attention is given to the problem of 'peak oil,' the geopolitical implications of water shortages are only recently being realised. Yet despite the major dislocations that could be caused by the alleged problems of the 'peak oil' scenario for our industrial societies, there are alternative energy options; however, there is no substitute for water, the very substance of life itself.

China's domination of Tibet is the key to understanding an approaching geopolitical crisis. The domination of Tibet means that China controls the Himalayan headwaters of the main rivers of India and Southeast Asia that provide sustenance to the agriculture and energy of these immense territories. With China facing problems of irrigation and drought, the Beijing leadership is unlikely to hesitate to use the Himalayan headwaters in whatever manner they deem apt for China's interests. When faced with any question as to China's interests, especially in regard to territory and resources, the façade of good neighbourliness quickly drops, as in the example of China's ongoing territorial disputes with Japan, Vietnam and India.

---

5   *Rival*. Dictionary.com. *Online Etymology Dictionary*, http://dictionary.reference. com/browse/rival.

It is Asia's other emerging superpower, India, that will likely become the focus of an emerging regional conflict with China. Since the Chinese invasion of Tibet there have been border disputes with India, but it is China's control over the headwaters of rivers that flow into India from Tibet that provides the key to understanding the source of this potential regional conflict. The ongoing territorial disagreement between China and India could be but the prelude to a far more serious dispute should China proceed with plans to divert the water sources she controls in Tibet in ways that would benefit China at India's expense.

China's border disputes with India during the period of 1960–62 left 3,000 Indians dead: and China still claims the entire Indian state of Arunachal Pradesh, which borders southern Tibet. India in turn protests that China is occupying 15,000 square miles of what she claims is Indian territory in Akasi Chin high in the Himalayas. Chinese intransigence in relation to India continues to be played out in diplomatic confrontations, as shown in ongoing negotiations over the disputed areas between China and India.

A thirteenth round of negotiations between India and China, on 7 and 8 August 2009, between China's delegation, led by special representative State Councillor Dai Bingguo, and an Indian delegation led by National Security Adviser M. K. Narayanan, was intended to work out specific details on how to proceed with negotiations on border demarcation and delineation. In other words, although the border talks had begun in 2003, the basis for negotiations has still not even been agreed upon. There was much emphasis on the cordial atmosphere and a 'shared vision' between the two Asian powers,[6] yet India and China continue to build up forces along the disputed border area.

Despite the political rhetoric about the 'shared vision'

---

6   Sandeep Dikshit, 'India China to Start Up Hotline,' *The Hindu*, 9 August 2009, 1.

between China and India arising from this 13th round of talks as stated in Government press releases[7] both powers remain in a state of permanent tension over a number of issues that are likely to be exacerbated in the near future. For instance, even the current world financial recession resulted in a ban on some Chinese imports,[8] despite China's being India's largest trading partner, upon which the basis of any relaxed Sino-India relations must exist. In April 2009 Beijing blocked a $US 2.9 billion Asian Development Bank (ADB) loan to India that included $US 60 million for a flood control project in the disputed Arunachal Pradesh. External Affairs Minister S. M. Krishna stated that India would not in the future be 'putting her palm out' for funding from international agencies but would use internal sources.[9]

In June 2009, the Indian Government announced the deployment of an additional 60,000 soldiers, along with tanks and two squadrons of advanced SU-30MKI strike aircraft, to the northeast state of Assam, near Arunachal Pradesh, bringing the total troop numbers in the area to 100,000.[10]

---

7   'Manmohan Singh Says India Committed to Promote Its Relations With China,' *Thaindian News*, 1 October 2009, http://74.125.155.132/ search?q=cache:sRUHaAtkXYwJ:www.thaindian.com/newsportal/india-news/ manmohan-singh-says-india-committed-to-promote-its-relations-with-china_100254569.html.

8   This involved a ban on toys from China, an action that had significant economic consequences. China makes the majority of the world's toys of which India imports 350 million pounds annually. It has been suggested the real reason for the ban was in retaliation for China's growing links with Pakistan. Malcolm Moore, 'China Outraged After India Bans All Toy Imports,' *Daily Telegraph*, 4 February 2009, http://www.telegraph.co.uk/finance/financetopics/recession/4511451/China-outraged-after-India-bans-all-toy-imports.html.

9   'India to Finance 'Sensitive' Areas' Projects Itself: Krishna,' *Thaindian News*, 17 August 2009, http://www.thaindian.com/newsportal/uncategorized/india-to-finance-sensitive-areas-projects-itself-krishna_100233891.html.

10 John Cherion, 'China Bogey,' *Frontline: India's National Magazine*, vol. 26, no. 21, 10–23 October 2009, http://74.125.155.132/ search?q=cache:pHCY8ETII2MJ:www.hinduonnet.com/fline/ stories/20091023262103700.htm.

In response, China's official *Global Times* published an editorial on 9 June 2009 warning India 'to consider whether or not it can afford the consequences of a potential confrontation with China.' The editorial reminded India that China had established close relations with Pakistan, Sri Lanka and Nepal, and declared: 'China won't make any compromises in its border disputes with India.'[11] Despite the economic changes, and the 'openness' of China as being a new member of the 'world community,' nothing has fundamentally changed in the outlook of the Chinese leadership from the Mao era in regard to territory and superpower bullying.

In this regard, China saw the ADB loan to India for the development of Arunachal Pradesh as a direct challenge. An unnamed Chinese official told the *South China Morning Post* on 7 August 2009 that India had intensified the border row with China by obtaining the ADB funding through the support of the US and Japan. The official is quoted as stating: 'India has enough money to develop Arunachal Pradesh. But it wanted to test the Chinese. China opposed the loan application tooth and nail but India had its way. We lost face. And we don't like losing face. We disgrace anyone who disgraces us.'

Both India and China are becoming increasingly belligerent. China's ambassador to India, Zhang Yan, urged both sides to resolve their disputes 'with the utmost political wisdom.' Professor Brahma Chellaney responded in the *Indian Express*:

---

11 'India's Unwise Military Moves,' *Global Times*, 9 June 2009, cited in: *Pak Tribune*, 'Cow (India) Desire of Hitting Bull (China),' 10 August 2009, http://74.125.155.132/search?q=cache:5VOcJaMz9MgJ:www.paktribune.com/news/index.php. The *Paktribune* article also cites a further Chinese article, stating: 'An affiliate of the *People's Daily* published a Chinese language article on June 12 which translates to "India is a paper tiger and its use of force will be trounced, say experts."'

Mr. Zhang's syrupy words are designed to salvage the [border] negotiations from the damage inflicted by vituperative attacks on India in China's state-run media. China's objective is to keep India engaged in endless and fruitless border talks so that Beijing, in the meantime, can change the Himalayan balance decisively in its favour through development of military power and infrastructure.[12]

In 2006, China built a major railway into the Tibetan plateau.[13] This was generally perceived by Indian officials and defence analysts as intended for the rapid deployment of troops to attack India. Indian strategist Dr. Brahma Chellaney[14] speaks of the rail system in military terms: 'The $6.2 billion Gormu-Lhasa railway, . . . has significantly augmented China's rapid military-deployment capability against India just when Beijing is becoming increasingly assertive in its claims on Indian territories. . . .'[15]

China has also been constructing a so-called 'string of pearls' of ports and other facilities for warships in the Indian Ocean. These naval constructions have caused concern in New Delhi about China's intrusion into India's 'backyard.' In response, India is building up her own naval power. A week prior to

---

12   Quoted in *The South China Morning Post*, 'China and India Resume Talks Over Disputed Border,' 7 August 2009, 6.

13   Joseph Kahn, Last Stop, 'Lhasa: Rail Link Ties Remote Tibet to China,' *The New York Times*, 2 July 2006, http://www.nytimes.com/2006/07/02/world/asia/02tibet. html.

14   Brahma Chellaney is one of India's most eminent strategy analysts, serving as Professor of Strategic Studies at the New Delhi-based think tank, the Centre for Policy Research. He was a Member of the Policy Advisory Group headed by the External Affairs Minister of India. Chellaney was an adviser to India's National Security Council until January 2000, serving as convenor of the External Security Group of the National Security Advisory Board, and a member of the Board's Nuclear Doctrine Group.

15   Brahma Chellaney, 'View: Sino-Indian Water Divide,' *Pakistan Daily Times*, 4 August 2009, http://www.dailytimes.com.pk/default.asp?page=2009\08\04\ story_4-8-2009_pg3_3.

the 7 and 8 August 2009 China-India talks on Arunachal Pradesh, the Indian defence ministry's naval planner, Alok Bhatnagar, announced that India would build 107 warships over the next decade, including aircraft carriers, destroyers, frigates and nuclear submarines, to rival China's fleet. Bhatnagar stated: 'China is developing its navy at a great rate. Its ambitions in the Indian Ocean are quite clear.'[16] A week later Chinese and Indian officials were publicly enthusing over the cordial and cooperative atmosphere that supposedly pervaded the Arunachal Pradesh talks, albeit the 13th round that again got nothing resolved.

Meanwhile, 'India has this year moved two army divisions to areas adjacent to the border with China, and built three new airstrips in the Himalayan foothills. The build-up is seen as a bid to match Chinese military might in southern Tibet, and to deter increasingly frequent cross-border incursions by Chinese patrols.'[17]

A flashpoint is Siachen Glacier on the India-Pakistan border. The small Himalayan village of Demchok has been the centre of recent Sino-Indian tension. Two Chinese helicopters flew close over the village in August 2009, proceeding several miles into Indian territory.[18] This has prompted New Delhi to change its policy and begin developing infrastructure along the neglected Himalayan foothills, the lack of development having been a strategy to slow down a possible Chinese invasion.

---

16   'India Plans to Build 100 Warships, Work on 32 Vessels Already Under Way,' *The Nation*, 31 July 2009, http://74.125.155.132/search?q=cache:A4rvAzhM4tsJ:www.nation.com.pk/pakistan-news-newspaper-daily-english-online/International/31-Jul-2009/India-plans-to-build-100-warships-work-on-32-vessels-already-under-way--.

17   Peter Ford, 'Rivals China, India in Escalating War of Words,' *The Christian Science Monitor*, 20 October 2009, http://www.csmonitor.com/2009/1020/p06s04-woap.html.

18   Ben Arnoldy, 'Growing Number of China Incursions Into India Lead to a Strategy Change,' *The Christian Science Monitor*, 29 September 2009, http://www.csmonitor.com/2009/0929/p06s06-wosc.html.

But in response to a major spike in cross-border incursions by the Chinese in the past few years, the Indian approach is changing, with plans to expand infrastructure and bring more of a government footprint to the contested region.

'Now the Chinese are basically doing so much damage on the Tibetan plateau, and given these Chinese border incidents and provocations, the Indians have been left with no choice but to begin infrastructure development along the Himalayas,' says Mr. Chellaney.[19]

Chellaney states that Chinese incursions over this border area increased from 140 in 2007 to 280 in 2008.[20] '"That is alarming. That means the Chinese are still sustaining pressure at last year's level," says Chellaney.'[21]

In September 2009, the Indian Air Force opened a high-altitude airfield in the Ladakh district of India's far north, which shares borders with China and Pakistan. Two other airfields were built in the Himalayas over the 15 previous months, including the world's highest at 16,200 feet at Daulat Beg Oldi.

India is currently repositioning Sukhoi war jets to its north-eastern borders with China. Air Chief Marshal P. V. Naik said earlier this month that while the Chinese posed no imminent threat, there was a jet gap.

'Our present aircraft strength is inadequate. Aircraft strength is one third that of China. The government of India is doing a lot to augment Air Force capability,' he said.[22]

---

19 Ibid.
20 Ibid.
21 Ibid.
22 Ibid.

The combination of China, India and Pakistan as nuclear powers provides for a volatile mix. China attempted to block India's access to the Nuclear Supplies Group after a civil nuclear deal between a US firm and India went ahead under the former Bush administration.[23] China provides nuclear and other military assistance to Pakistan. This is widely perceived to be a reflection of superpower suspicion between the US and China, with the US using India in a balance of power strategy for the region. However, it is more likely that the US is attempting to woo India away from her historic relationship with Russia, whose aspirations under the post-Yeltsin regimes have been of major concern to US global power elites,[24] which do not wish to see a return of a 'poliverse'[25] in world affairs.

During US Secretary of State Hillary Clinton's trip to India in July 2009, she signed a defence pact for expanding US

---

23 Ratified by US Congress, 1 October 2008. The nuclear treaty with the US might more cynically be viewed as a means of restraining India while China has no such restraints. The Treaty places India's nuclear energy development under the scrutiny of the United Nations' International Atomic Energy Association (IAEA), and reaffirms India's continued moratorium on nuclear weapons testing.
'India works toward negotiating a Fissile Material Cut-off Treaty (FMCT) with the United States banning the production of fissile material for weapons purposes. India agrees to prevent the spread of enrichment and reprocessing technologies to states that don't possess them and to support international non-proliferation efforts.' Esther Pan and Jayshree Bajoria, *Backgrounder: The U.S.-India Nuclear Deal*, Council on Foreign Relations, 2 October 2008, http://www.cfr.org/publication/9663/.

24 http://groups.yahoo.com/group/WarOnFreedom/message/4141
In an interview with Radio Free Europe/Radio Liberty in 2005, Zbigniew Brzezinski of the Washington Center for Strategic and International Studies, National Security Adviser under the Carter presidency and a key foreign policy adviser to President Obama, was frank about the subversive activity being directed against Russia by the US: 'The United States is supporting and de facto promoting geopolitical pluralism in the space of the [former] Soviet Union.' 'U.S./Russia: Zbigniew Brzezinski Assesses U.S.-Russia Relations,' 11 May 2005, http://www.rferl.org/content/article/1058818.html (accessed 30 October 2009).

25 'Poliverse' is a term used by leading Russian geopolitical theorist Dr. A. G. Dugin, director of the Center for Conservative Studies, Moscow State University, in explaining the aim of creating a global order based on a number of geopolitical 'vectors,' as opposed to global hegemony by one or two superpowers. This 'poliverse' would comprise self-contained geopolitical blocs. See A. G. Dugin, 'The Eurasian Idea,' *Ab Aeterno*, no. 1, November 2009.

arms sales to India, including fighters and other high-tech weapons.[26] In July 2009, India launched her first nuclear-powered submarine armed with nuclear missiles, making her the sixth country with these weapons systems.[27]

The relationship between Russia and China extends back to a visit by Indian Prime Minister Jawaharlal Nehru to the Soviet Union in June 1955 and Khrushchev's return trip to India in 1955. The USSR remained neutral during the border confrontations between China and India in 1959 and 1962, despite the supposedly 'fraternal relations' existing between the two nominally communist states and the 'friendship treaty' (*sic*) existing between the USSR and China.

In 1962 the Soviet Union agreed to transfer technology to co-produce the MiG-21 jet fighter in India, which the USSR had previously denied to China.

Indo-Russian military cooperation is not limited to the sale of weaponry. Military cooperation extends to joint research and development, training, service-to-service contacts, and includes joint exercises such as the joint naval exercises that took place in April 2007 in the Sea of Japan and the joint airborne exercises held in September 2007 in Russia.

A few months after the nuclear energy treaty between the US and India, in December 2008 Russia and India signed an agreement to build civilian nuclear reactors in India during a visit by the Russian president to New Delhi.[28]

---

26 'India, US Agree Nuclear Sites, Defense Pact,' *China Daily*, 21 July 2009, http://www.chinadaily.com.cn/cndy/2009-07/21/content_8451977.htm.

27 Lydia Pollgreen, 'India Launches Nuclear Submarine,' *New York Times*, 26 July 2000.

28 Among the many agreements signed by President Medvedev on his state visit to India were the *Agreement on Construction of Additional Nuclear Plants at Kudankulum site as well as Construction of Russian-designed Nuclear Power Plants at New Sites within Republic of India*. See: Dr. Subhash Kapila, Russia: 'President Medvedev's visit to India' (December 2008) reviewed, Paper No. 2978, 10 December 2008. This includes, as an appendix to the entire Indo-Russian

This indicates the low regard India gives to any treaty with the US designed to wooing India away from her historic relationship with Russia.

Under the Integrated Long-Term Programme (ILTP) of cooperation between Russia and India, India's Department of Science and Technology and Russia's Academy of Sciences and Ministry of Industry, Science and Technology are coordinated. Joint ventures under ILTP include development of SARAS Duet aircraft, semiconductor products, supercomputers, poly-vaccines, laser science and technology, seismology, high-purity materials, software and IT. There are many other important areas of Indo-Russian cooperation, including those of space and energy.

That India does not intend to align with the US at the expense of her relationship with Russia is indicated by a ten-year military pact between Russia and India formalised in October 2009. *The Hindu* reported of the pact:

> The new programme of military-technical cooperation during 2011–2020 will cover both ongoing projects— such as the Su-30 MKI fighter plane and the T-90 tank production in India—as well as 31 new projects, Defence Minister A. K. Antony said. He co-chaired with Russian Defence Minister Anatoly Serdyukov the ninth session of the Indo-Russian Inter-Governmental Commission on Military Technical Cooperation (IRIGC-MTC), which met here on Wednesday and Thursday. 'It will be a bigger programme than the current 10-year programme which expires next year, and will see a further shift from the buyer-seller relationship to joint design, development and production,' Mr. Antony said after the meeting.[29]

---

declaration: *Joint Declaration between the Republic of India and the Russian Federation During the Visit of the President of the Russian Federation* (5 December 2008). http://74.125.155.132/search?q=cache:Ot99UtWcFRIJ:www.southasiaanalysis. org/%255Cpapers30%255Cpaper2978.html

29   Vladimir Radyuhin, 'New 10-year Defence Tie-up with Russia Finalised,'

Indian Defence Minister Antony stated that the new projects under the 2020 programme would be the fifth-generation fighter aircraft, the Multirole Transport Aircraft, a new multirole helicopter and many other joint projects for the Army, the Navy and the Air Force. An *Inter-Governmental Agreement on After-Sales Product Support* would also be signed. Russia would speed up the delivery of 40 additional Su-30 MKIs commissioned by India and kits for 140 jets to be assembled in the country. 'Hitches in indigenous production of T-90 tanks in India were also resolved, Mr. Antony said. Russia would expedite the construction of 140 T-90 tanks for the Indian Army and transfer of technology for production under licence in India.'[30]

Indo-Russian defence ties were 'a unique partnership, as we do not have such a high-level defence cooperation arrangement with any other country,' Mr. Antony told Moscow-based Indian media. 'Even as we develop cooperative ties with other countries, they will not be at the expense of our time-tested friendship with Russia.' 'The Russian side shared this perception and that was why it was willing to expand and intensify bilateral defence cooperation.'[31]

A. K. Antony's comments are a clear message to the US that Indo-Russian friendship will remain firm regardless of any accords reached with the US or its allies. This is further indicated by a pact clearly aimed strategically at China and China-backed Pakistan, India's only real antagonists in the region, as indicated by the comment by Serdyukov: 'I am confident the agreements reached at this session will not only guarantee the success of our military-technical cooperation but will help maintain strategic stability in the region.'[32]

The Hindu, 16 October 2009, http://www.hindu.com/2009/10/16/
stories/2009101659881000.htm.

30 Ibid.

31 Ibid.

32 Ibid.

Offsetting the alliance between Russia and India are recent Chinese interventions in regard to Indo-Pakistani territorial issues. The new strategy from Beijing appears to be to use Pakistan as a proxy for the ever-present contention over Arunachal Pradesh. As noted previously, the 13th round of talks between India and China on this area were described in enthusiastic terms by both sides, which in reality mean nothing. Soon after the supposedly cordial talks, China offered to assist Pakistan to develop Arunachal Pradesh as a proxy occupying state. Peter Ford of the *Christian Science Monitor* reported that, 'The *People's Daily*, published by China's ruling Communist party, launched a blistering attack on India last week, accusing it in an editorial of "recklessness and arrogance" and of harbouring "the dream of superpower . . . mingled with the thought of hegemony."'[33]

The *People's Daily* comments followed a statement by the Chinese foreign ministry of its 'deep dissatisfaction' with the election campaign visit in October by Indian Prime Minister Manmohan Singh to Arunachal Pradesh.[34]

One Chinese response has been to offer 'aid for a hydro-power project in Pakistan-controlled Kashmir, which India claims as its own territory.'[35] The offer was met with diplomatic protest from India.

India's allowing the Dalai Lama to visit a major Tibetan monastery in Arunachal Pradesh in November 2009[36] can be seen in the context of this Indo-China rivalry.

Shen Dingli, deputy head of China's South Asia Research Institute, cogently expressed the real issue:

33   Peter Ford, 'Rivals China, India in Escalating War of Words.'
34   Ibid.
35   Ibid.
36   Ibid.

'The question is who leads in Asia?'[37] Indian Home Minister Palaniappan Chidambaram has stated: 'China is fishing in troubled waters.' Air Force Chief Fali Homi Major stated to the *Hindustan Times* that China is a 'greater threat' to India than Pakistan.[38]

Into this volatile mix of long-standing rivalry, border and territorial disputes, and US and Russian strategies, against the background as to who shall become the predominant power in Asia, exist numerous scenarios for natural disaster that would cause major demographic shifts and ultimately the potential for war. Just as the seething tensions that exist among Asian states are barely recognised by the West, so too the crucial problem of water resources is rarely understood. The basic life source of water has far greater potential to cause regional and continental havoc than problems of oil shortage.

CHINA'S WATER CRISIS AND DESERTIFICATION PROBLEMS

Drought and creeping desertification are major problems facing China, concerning which China has options that other Asian states, including India, do not have: namely, control over the headwaters of the main hydro sources for India and much of Southeast Asia, and even further afield into Central Asia and Russia. Obviously, if China faces catastrophic problems with water resources, it will act in its own interests regardless of what Beijing now states about 'shared visions' and being part of the 'world community.' Beijing's attitude is already clear as shown by construction plans for damming the Himalayan headwaters. The most vital of lifelines for much of Asia will therefore be subjected to Beijing's will, and years of diplomatic discussions are not going to solve immediate, pressing problems of mass famine.

Northern China persistently faces drought. Henan, the centre of China's food production, issued a drought red alert on 5 February 2009. Xinhua, the official Chinese news agency, stated: 'The provincial meteorological bureau said the drought is the worst since 1951. The drought has affected about 63 percent of the province's 78.9 million mu (5.26 million hectares) of wheat.'[39] Other provinces put on 'red alert' in 2009 include Anhui and Shanxi, where approximately one million people and 160,000 heads of livestock face water shortages. Other provinces affected by drought include Hebei, Jiangsu and Shandong. Chinese reports stated that the drought threatened about 43 percent of the China's winter wheat supplies.[40] In 2009 nearly a million Chinese endured drought in east China, due to the lowering of water levels of four of the province's five rivers. The *Shanghai Daily* stated:

A drought since September had affected 909,000 people in east China's Jiangxi Province, a spokesman for the provincial flood control and drought relief office said yesterday. The drought had cut off normal water supplies in some rural areas. 'Villagers in Fengxin, Jing'an and Leping counties have to carry drinking water by trucks,' said Sun Xiaoshan, deputy director of the office. 'The water levels of four of the province's five main rivers hit record lows and are still dropping. The self-cleaning ability of rivers has decreased significantly due to the drastic fall of volume, posing a threat to public health.' The provincial government had stepped up monitoring and supervision over enterprises that may cause pollution, Sun added. The drought was expected to end

39 *Fire Earth: Environmental Issues*, 'Drought: China's Arch Nemesis,' 26 February 2009, http://feww.wordpress.com/2009/02/06/.
40 Ibid.

between January and February, he said.[41]

The Chinese news service Xinhuanet reported that, 'Investigations show that China has 2.62 million square kilometres of areas under desertification, double the total farmland in the country,' according to Lu Qi, a researcher with China Research and Development Center for Prevention and Control on Desertification.[42] A 2009 report cited by the Xinhua official news agency stated that, 'About 35% of China's agricultural land is affected by desertification seriously threatening its ability to feed its population, a nationwide survey revealed. . . . About 1.6 million square km of land are being degraded by water erosion each year affecting almost every river basin. Additionally, 2.0 million square km are eroded by wind,' the report states.[43]

INDIA'S WATER TABLE DEPLETION

India faces a major problem with its water table shrinkage. A report by hydrologists from NASA's Gravity Recovery and Climate Experiment (GRACE) Earth Science Team states that water is being pumped and consumed faster than the aquifers can be replenished through natural mechanisms.[44]

The team found that Northern India's water tables have fallen by approximately a fifth more than expected because of excessive use. Dr. Rodell, who led the study, stated that, 'If measures are not taken to ensure sustainable groundwater usage, consequences for the 114 million residents of the

41 '909,000 Hit by Drought,' *ShanghaiDaily.com*, 7 November 2009, http://www.shanghaidaily.com/sp/article/2009/200911/20091107/article_418742.htm.

42 Xinhuanet official news agency, 'China Suffers Great Losses from Desertification,' 17 June 2003. 'China Is Losing 4.5 billion Tons of Soil Each Year'; cited by Reuters, 'China's Crops at Risk from Massive Erosion,' 21 November 2008, http://www.reuters.com/article/environmentNews/idUSTRE4AK1J220081121?sp=true.

43 Ibid.

44 NASA: 'NASA Hydrologist Matt Rodell Discusses Vanishing Groundwater in India,' 12 August 2009, http://www.nasa.gov/topics/earth/features/india_water.html.

region may include a collapse of agricultural output and severe shortages of potable water.' Groundwater across the three northern Indian states of Rajasthan, Punjab and Haryan has dropped by about 4cm a year between 2002 and 2008. The Team report states that, 'The northern Indian states of Rajasthan, Punjab and Haryana have all of the ingredients for groundwater depletion: staggering population growth, rapid economic development and water-hungry farms, which account for about 95 percent of groundwater use in the region.'[45]

An increasing percentage of India's groundwater is unsuitable both for drinking and irrigation. The water is being pumped mainly for the irrigation of cropland, but faster than the aquifers (cavities and layers of porous rock, gravel, sand, or clay) can be replenished naturally. 'This illustrates that degraded water quality can contribute to water scarcity as it limits its availability for both human use and the ecosystem.'[46] Bridget Scanlon, a hydrologist at the Jackson School of Geosciences at the University of Texas in Austin, comments, 'That cycle is now overwhelming fresh water reserves all over the world. Even one region's water problem has implications beyond its borders.'[47]

CHINA'S CONTROL OF ASIA'S WATER SOURCES

Dr. Brahma Chellaney, in a detailed article for the *Japan Times*,[48] gives an authoritative account of the water crises confronting Asia, especially in relation to China and India, writing:

45   Ibid.

46   Ibid.

47   Ibid.

48   Brahma Chellaney, 'China Aims for Bigger Share of South Asia's Water Lifeline,' *Japan Times*, 26 June 2007, http://search.japantimes.co.jp/cgi-bin/eo20070626bc. html.

Water shortages in much of Asia are beginning to threaten rapid economic modernization, prompting the building of upstream projects on international rivers. If water geopolitics were to spur interstate tensions through reduced water flows to neighbouring states, the Asian renaissance could stall.

Water has emerged as a key issue that could determine whether Asia is headed toward mutually beneficial cooperation or deleterious interstate competition. No country could influence that direction more than China, which controls the Tibetan plateau—the source of most major rivers of Asia.[49]

Chellaney states that Tibet has the world's greatest river systems due to its vast glaciers and high altitude. Chellaney describes the extent and significance of this water source:

Tibet's vast glaciers and high altitude have endowed it with the world's greatest river systems. Its river waters are a lifeline to the world's two most-populous states— China and India—as well as to Bangladesh, Myanmar, Bhutan, Nepal, Cambodia, Pakistan, Laos, Thailand and Vietnam. These countries make up 47 percent of the global population.[50]

Although it has over half the world's population, Asia has less fresh water than any continent other than Antarctica. Chellaney refers to a 'looming struggle,' and to 'the spectre of water wars in Asia . . . being highlighted by climate change and environmental degradation in the form of shrinking forests and swamps, which foster a cycle of chronic flooding and droughts through the depletion of nature's water storage and absorption cover.'[51]

---

49   Ibid.

50   Ibid.

51   Ibid.

Chellaney points out that there should be greater concern 'for the potential interstate conflict over river-water resources'[52] where disputes have already become rife in several Asian states from India and Pakistan to Southeast Asia and China:

> This concern arises from Chinese attempts to dam or redirect the southward flow of river waters from the Tibetan plateau, where major rivers originate, including the Indus, the Mekong, the Yangtze, the Yellow, the Salween, the Brahmaputra, the Karnali and the Sutlej. Among Asia's mighty rivers, only the Ganges starts from the Indian side of the Himalayas.[53]

The problems with irrigation for agriculture in northern and eastern China, as already discussed, have obliged China to focus on the water sources it controls in Tibet, and is already starting to dam rivers not only for hydropower but for diverting waters for irrigation and other purposes. Having already built two dams up the Mekong, China is building at least three more, provoking alarm from Vietnam, Laos, Cambodia and Thailand. The vast projects that are reportedly intended for west-central Tibet that will disrupt the river water flows into India are proceeding while information from Beijing on these remains sparse.[54]

There are ten major watersheds formed by the Himalayas and Tibetan highlands, which spread river waters throughout Asia. 'Control over the 2.5 million-square-km Tibetan plateau gives China tremendous leverage, besides access to vast natural resources,' states Dr. Chellaney. 'Having extensively contaminated its own major rivers through unbridled industrialization, China now threatens the ecological viability of river systems tied to South and

52   Ibid.
53   Ibid.
54   Ibid.

Southeast Asia in its bid to meet its thirst for water and energy,' he writes.[55]

Perhaps few recognise the geopolitical significance of Tibet.[56] Apart from its immense mineral resources, Chellaney points out that China for the first time 'has a contiguous frontier with India, Myanmar, Bhutan and Nepal.'[57]

A blueprint for the rerouting of the waters of the Brahmaputra has been set out by a group of ex-officials, entitled *Tibet's Waters Will Save China*. Chellaney described the book as 'officially blessed.' In an update on the water issue, Dr. Chellaney writes of the Brahmaputra that:

It is the world's highest river, and also one of the fastest-flowing. Diversion of the Brahmaputra's water to the parched Yellow River is an idea that China does not discuss in public, because the project implies environmental devastation of India's northeastern plains and eastern Bangladesh, and would thus be akin to a declaration of water war on India and Bangladesh.[58]

Chellaney considers the rerouting of the Brahmaputra as a certainty:

The issue now is not whether China will reroute the Brahmaputra, but when. Once authorities complete their feasibility studies and the diversion scheme begins, the project will be presented as a fait accompli. China

---

55 Ibid.

56 In the numerous campaigns conducted by human rights activists against the Chinese occupation of Tibet, and the reports on the subject in the news media, little attention seems to have been given to Tibet's importance in terms of geopolitics, water and mineral resources. It seems to be the general view that control over Tibet is simply a matter of Chinese pride. China is not about to relinquish control over Tibet under any circumstances. Tibet is crucial to China's survival.

57 Chellaney, op. cit.

58 Ibid.

already has identified the bend where the Brahmaputra forms the world's longest and deepest canyon—just before entering India—as the diversion point.[59]

Chellaney considers that China 'seems intent on aggressively pursuing projects and employing water as a weapon. The idea of a Great South-North Water Transfer Project diverting river waters cascading from the Tibetan highlands had the backing of then President Hu Jintao . . .' He goes on to say:

> The Chinese ambition to channel the Brahmaputra waters to the parched Yellow River has been whetted by what Beijing touts as its engineering feat in building the giant $25 billion Three Gorges Dam project, which has officially displaced a staggering 1.2 million citizens. While China's water resources minister told a Hong Kong University meeting last October that, in his personal opinion, the idea to divert waters seems not viable, the director of the Yellow River Water Conservancy Committee said publicly that the mega-plan enjoys official sanction and may begin by 2010.[60]

China is clearly being duplicitous in its public pronouncements about its intentions in regard to the Brahmaputra. Past and present actions indicate that Beijing expects to get its own way over any disputes regarding territory and resources, and China is not about to back down or 'lose face' on one of the most vital issues of survival.

Dr. Chellaney states that the first phase of China's South-North Project involves building 300 km of tunnels and channels to draw waters from the Jinsha, Yalong and Dadu rivers, on the eastern rim of the Tibetan plateau. In the second phase the Brahmaputra waters would be directed northward.[61]

---

59   Ibid.
60   Ibid.
61   Ibid.

Most of Asia's major rivers—the Yellow, Yangzi, Mekong, Salween, Irrawaddy, Brahmaputra, Ganges, Sutlej, and Indus rivers—draw on the glaciers and snowmelt of the Himalayas. Except for the Ganges, the source for these rivers is in Tibet. The diversion of the Yalong Zangbo/ Brahmaputra, which would impact on Eastern India and Bangladesh, with a combined population larger than North China's, could be devastating. 'The potential for such a project to create conflicts between China and India—and to exacerbate existing conflicts over shared waterways between India and Bangladesh—is gigantic,' states Kenneth Pomeranz.[62]

CENTRAL ASIA

This conflict over water, while most obviously affecting the relations between India and China and further afield into South-east Asia, also has major consequences in Central Asia and potentially also draws China into conflict with Russia.

The Irtysh River, which shares borders with China, Russia, and Kazakhstan, places relations between these states in the same predicament as that between India and China over the Brahmaputra. Despite China's assurances, like Beijing's dubious assurances over the Brahmaputra, in regard to the Irtysh, Marat Yermukanov, a journalist for the Russian-language newspaper *Panorama Nedely* in Petropavlovsk, North Kazakhstan, writes: 'Patience ran out when Beijing started construction of a canal linking the Black Irtysh with the Karamai River on Chinese territory, dramatically lowering the water level in the river. China's water-management policy threatens to drastically reduce crop production in the environmentally vulnerable regions of

---

62   Kenneth Pomeranz, 'The Great Himalayan Watershed: Water Shortages, Mega-Projects and Environmental Politics in China, India, and Southeast Asia,' *The Asia-Pacific Journal*, vol. 30, 27 July 2009.

East Kazakhstan, Pavlodar, and Karaganda.'[63] Yermukanov added that, 'Such a move could also cause a severe drought in Russia's wheat-growing Omsk region.'

In November 2005, in a desperate attempt to prevent an environmental disaster, the Governor of the Omsk region, Leonid Polezhayev, ordered 10 billion roubles to be allocated for the construction of a huge water reservoir to accumulate floodwaters for industrial use. He argued that a political solution to the Irtysh River dispute was not feasible, since the Chinese did not wish to negotiate.[64]

In a situation similar to that of the negotiations between India and China over disputed territory, Russian Sinologists consider China to be stalling in talks over the Irtysh-Ili basin.[65]

Again, as with Chinese control over the Himalayan headwaters and widespread suspicion as to China's intentions in regard to damming and diverting these water sources, China has been exploiting the Ili River without regard to the concerns of Kazakhstan. In 2004 China opened a hydroelectric power station that consumes 15% of the Ili River's water resources, 65 hydroelectric power stations having already been built on the river, with plans for China to build another 13 reservoirs.[66] Bobo Lo, Senior Research Fellow and Director of the Russia and China programmes at the Centre for European Reform, states that many in the Kazakh Government are not even aware of the extent of China's hydro projects:

---

63 Marat Yermukanov, 'China Obstructs River Management Talks with Kazakhstan,' 17 February 2006; *Eurasia Daily Monitor*, Jamestown Foundation, http://jamestown.org/edm/article.php?article_id=2370793.
    The Jamestown Foundation is a US-based think tank specialising in the analysis of the affairs of the republics of the former USSR, and is staffed by academic specialists. *Eurasia Daily Monitor* is the Foundation's publication.

64 Yermukanov, op. cit., citing *Izvestiya Kazakhstan*, 14 February 2005.

65 Ibid.

66 Bobo Lo, 'Russia-China: Axis of Convenience,' 20 May 2008, http://www.opendemocracy.net/user/511394, citing: *Novoye pokolenie*, 10 February 2005.

. . . Environmentalists warn that in the next few years China will build additional hydroelectric power installations along the Irtysh and Ili Rivers. Among the installations not revealed to the Kazakh government delegation is the Kapshagay (a hydroelectric power station in Kazakhstan carries the same name) water reservoir, with the enormous capacity of 380 million cubic meters.[67]

Yermukanov refers to the polluting of Lake Balkhash by the industrialisation of northwestern China, and to the increased food production in Xingjiang Uighur. He points to Chinese mismanagement, and to the refusal of China to sign an agreement on shared water resources. The increase of rice production in the Xingjiang Uighur Autonomous Region has already resulted in the depletion of the Irtysh and Ili rivers. Yermukanov refers to the mismanagement of the Chinese section of the Ili river basin causing the loss of 4.4 cubic kilometres, which constituting 15% of the water resources of the river as a whole. 'That reduces substantially the amount of water inflow into Lake Balkhash,' Yermukanov writes. 'The root cause of the problem is that until now China had not signed the international convention on trans-border waters.'[68]

The international convention on water use referred to by Yermukanov is that of *The Convention on the Protection and Use of Transboundary Watercourses and International Lakes* ('Water Convention'), signed on 17 March 1992. The Convention obliges Parties to prevent, control and reduce water pollution from point and non-point sources. The Convention has provisions for monitoring, research and development, consultations, warning and alarm systems, mutual assistance, institutional arrangements, and the exchange and protection of information, as well as public

---

67   Ibid.
68   Yermukanov, op. cit.

access to information.[1] China's refusal to sign any such agreement makes her intentions suspect.

Aggravating the misuse of the Irtysh and Ili rivers, China also has territorial claims against Kazakhstan. Yermukanov states that despite border agreements between Kazakhstan and China, 'Beijing did not abandon altogether territorial claims on some southern regions of Kazakhstan. Some years ago a Kazakh Foreign Ministry delegation was surprised to see the former capital, Almaty, Balkhash, and other areas of south Kazakhstan marked as parts of China on a map in Beijing's central museum. The Foreign Ministry of Kazakhstan filed an official protest, and the Chinese promised to correct the mistake. But the school text on Xingjiang history lists the same parts of Kazakhstan as Chinese territory.'[2]

UN WORRIES OVER POTENTIAL FOR 'WATER WARS'

UN Secretary-General Ban Ki-moon has expressed concern about the disputes over water between states in the Middle East. At the 2007 Asia-Pacific Water Summit Ban Ki-moon stated that, 'Our planet faces a growing water crisis. But the situation in the Asia-Pacific region is especially troubling. High population growth, unsustainable consumption, pollution and poor management all threaten the area's clean water sources.'[3]

A 2009 UNESCO report, *Water in a Changing World*, refers to the need for urgent action if a 'global water crisis' is to be avoided.[4] Indeed, the UNESCO report places water

1   http://www.unece.org/env/water/
2   Ibid.
3   United Nations media release, 'Secretary General to Inaugural Asia-Pacific Water Summit,' 3 December 2007, http://www.un.org/News/Press/docs/2007/sgsm11311. doc.htm (accessed 28 October 2009).
4   The 3rd United Nations World Water Development Report, UNESCO, *Water in a*

problems at the centre of potential crises leading to national and even global conflicts:

> Water is linked to the crises of climate change, energy and food supplies and prices, and troubled financial markets. Unless their links with water are addressed and water crises around the world are resolved, these other crises may intensify and local water crises may worsen, converging into a global water crisis and leading to political insecurity and conflict at various levels.[5]

As to the present-day situation, all the diplomacy and alliances in regard to BRIC and the rest have not altered China's resolve an iota to control the headwaters of Asia. The clearest thinking on these problems continues to come from Brahma Chellaney, who has written of managing the rise of an increasingly assertive China as Asia's biggest challenge. This, he states, is highlighted by the unveiling of plans to construct dams on major rivers flowing to China's neighbours. China shares land and sea frontiers with twenty states. The major concern for many of these states is the manner by which China has unilaterally proceeded to control the water sources at the Tibetan plateau and Xinjiang, 're-engineering cross-border flows through dams, reservoirs, barrages, irrigation networks,' etc. This, states Chellaney, makes China a 'hydro-hegemon.' Asia is the world's driest continent in terms of *per capita* freshwater availability, states Chellaney, but China has refused to enter into any water-sharing treaties or regulatory frameworks, 'because it wants to maintain its strategic grip on trans-boundary river flows.' The Salween, running from Tibet through Yunnan Province into Burma and Thailand, will cease to be Asia's last largely free-flowing river, with work on the 4,200-megawatt Songta Dam in Tibet due to begin soon. Other newly approved

---

Changing World, March 2009.

5   *Water in a Changing World*, ibid., Overview of key messages, xx, http://www.unesco. org/water/wwap/wwdr/wwdr3/pdf/08_WWDR3_overview_of_key_msgs.pdf.

dam projects will be on Brahmaputra, and the Mekong, six already having been built on the Mekong, which is crucial to the Southeast Asia; while Brahmaputra supplies northeast Indian and Bangladesh.[6]

What can be stated with relative confidence is that it won't be the United Nations or any other such international organisation, treaty or agreement that will forestall or avert crises resulting from the competition for water resources. As stated, China has shown no inclination to binding itself to any international agreement regarding water resources. China, despite becoming part of the so-called 'world community' and its talk of 'shared visions' with India, Russia and other neighbours, has not repudiated or even compromised on the old territorial claims that have persisted since Mao and before. There seems little optimism for expecting an altruistic or 'neighbourly' attitude from China towards its neighbours if survival depends upon exploiting and diverting water resources at the expense of others.

Power, Famine and Erosion

While I contend that conflicts over water resources could be a pivotal factor in determining the shape and future of the Indo-Pacific region and its alliances, there are other scenarios, any one or a combination of which could trigger the fragmenting of tenuous geopolitical relationships.

Chinese economic expansion is running amok, as the Communists have embarked on a 'market economy' aligned with Western capital and technology. The Chinese economy is a juggernaut that threatens to consume everything in its path and ultimately implode. Other economies, including the US, are intent on hitching themselves to the Chinese

---

6   Brahma Chellaney, 'Asia's Dammed Water Hegemon,' Project Syndicate, 5 March 2013, http://www.project-syndicate.org/commentary/china-s-threat-to-regional-water-cooperation-by-brahma-chellaney.

star; however it is a shooting star that could easily come crushing to earth causing widespread devastation. While it is glowing and on the ascent, our politicians and businessmen are dazzled by the markets it is supposed to deliver. However, there are a number of factors that will eventually cause China to crash, taking sundry nations with it. In this situation China will resort to an aggressive policy rather than succumb.

ENERGY SHORTAGES

Chinese economic expansion is proceeding without regard to environmental impact, dwindling natural resources and availability of energy. As we shall see, China also faces a crisis in food production, and it is apparent that the associated environmental problems are given secondary regard relative to industrialisation. China's military expansion and strategic bases over the Pacific region, mostly undertaken under the pretext of economic and diplomatic relations with island nations, is preparation for war or military blackmail when faced with a crash.

A *New York Times* report from Shanghai in 2004 cogently explained China's predicament, stating, 'With the hottest days of summer fast approaching, Shanghai is making preparations to seed clouds over the city to make it rain, in the hope that a couple of degrees of reduced temperatures will help ward off brownouts, or worse, here in China's biggest city and commercial capital.'[7]

That year China projected a 20-million-kilowatt shortfall in electricity supplies, with severe power shortages predicted for the country's southern and eastern regions. 'Guangzhou, China's third-largest city, an industrial powerhouse, has had rationing since January, six months earlier than the

---

7   Howard W. French, 'Flaring Growth Puts China on Track for Burnout,' *New York Times*, 5 July 2004.

emergency measures put into effect last year.' The *New York Times*' journalist, Howard French, stated that the issue was one of 'whether the country's leaders can successfully continue to manage this huge and increasingly complex economy at growth rates that are among the world's fastest.' Significantly, he stated that 'the rush to find short-term palliatives for the country's immense power crunch, however, reflects creeping doubts of a more profound order.'

The worry, put bluntly, is that the world simply may not have enough energy and other resources for China to continue developing along present lines, especially at its present rate. Furthermore, sharply increased environmental damage might make the country unlivable, even if such growth could be sustained.

According to Zhang Jun, a prominent Chinese economist who has made a comparative study of China and India, China consumes three times as much energy and 15 times as much steel as its neighbor, even though the Chinese economy is only roughly twice the size, and is growing only about 10 percent faster than India's.

The toll on China's environment from this growth-at-any-cost strategy has been alarming. China's official development goal is to build what the government calls a well-off society by 2020, yet today the growth that makes such dreams permissible has left China with 16 of the world's 20 most polluted cities, according to the World Bank.[8]

Regardless of the problems of drought that plague China, water pollution is a major problem. 'The Chinese government says that 90 percent of urban residents face serious water pollution problems.' Most of the population—700 million—must drink contaminated water. 'Even the country's seas

8   Ibid.

are increasingly under siege from industrial pollution.'[9]

In 2011 there were power shortages partly because of flooding in one of China's major coal suppliers, Australia.[10] Conditions in Australia had major consequences in China, indicating the fragility of the interrelationships throughout the region, and how one disaster in one state can have major consequences far away. China faced the same situation of coal shortages in 2012.[11]

China is economically unviable, yet many states believe that China's mass consumer market and cheap labour provide panaceas for their own debt-ridden economies.

CLIMATIC CHANGES & CRISIS IN FOOD PRODUCTION

Global warming will result in major climatic changes in the Pacific and will have devastating consequences for China. In 1998 increased precipitation, more forceful monsoons and the snowpack melt runoff from high mountains caused the Yangtze basin to flood. 13.8 million people were driven from their homes. Crops were destroyed over 11 million acres, or 3% of the national cropland. That year summer floods affected 240 million people and submerged 54.2 million acres of farmland, according to the Chinese Ministry of Civil Affairs. Sufficient rice production is a major problem, with China often facing grain shortages. In 2003 production was 55 million tonnes less than consumption, prompting a dramatic rise in grain imports and resulting in across the board grain price rises on international markets. 'Shrinking acreages, falling water tables and a population

9   Ibid.

10   Dexter Roberts, 'China's Power Outages Come Early and Often,' *Bloomberg Businessweek*, 12 May 2011, http://www.businessweek.com/magazine/content/11_21/b4229011807240.htm.

11   Wang Yong, 'Power Shortage to Continue in 2012,' *CaixinOnline*, 7 February 2012, http://english.caixin.com/2012-02-07/100354067.html.

that is expected to grow significantly beyond 1.3 billion are factors that have led some grain experts to conclude that China will be a net food importer in coming years.'

Harvestable land declined by 6.7 million hectares since between 1996 and 2004, according to the Ministry of Land and Resources.[12] A Chinese Government report states that 'soil erosion is a serious problem in China, occurring on a much larger scale than in other developing countries.'

> Since the late 1940s, the eroded area has increased by 38 percent, and the area subject to erosion now includes nearly 18 million square kilometres, one-sixth of China's total land area. An additional 5 billion tons of topsoil is lost every year from the use of marginal lands for farming, deforestation, and intensive agriculture. This soil erosion has caused serious land degradation, loss of agricultural productivity and even exposure of the bedrock in some mountainous areas. It has also led to increased siltation of rivers and lakes and a greater frequency of floods, droughts, and landslides, posing tremendous costs in human lives and economic losses. As a result, over three-quarters of the poorest counties in China lie in areas suffering from severe soil erosion.[13]

Despite China's long history of soil erosion control and reclamation, 'the area of soil brought under control has been far exceeded by the size of newly-eroded areas.' The report states that 'in the Yangtze River valley, the newly-eroded areas are three times larger than the areas brought under control.[14] Indications are that China is not going to overcome these problems and warnings over the past

---

12   'Global rice industry report: *Oryza Market Report*, China, 19 July 2004.

13   'Prevention and Control of Soil Erosion and Land Degradation in the Middle and Upper Reaches of the Yangtze River,' Project Scope and Relationship to China's Agenda 21, acca21.org

14   Ibid.

few years are becoming ever more dire. In 2010 China's Ministry of Water Resources warned that if the current rate of soil erosion continued over the next 50 years there would be a 40 per cent decrease in food production. Already the total area of soil erosion has reached nearly 17 per cent of total land cover, putting in doubt the food security of one million people. More than 30 percent of China's counties are experiencing soil erosion.[15]

Decades ago, Harrison Salisbury presciently warned that a China faced with famine will not simply lie down and die, when the resources and lands of Russia—and other neighbours—beckon. Because China has entered the global economy since the death of Mao politicians and businessmen, short of clarity beyond immediate gain, imagine that China will never again resort to belligerence, regardless of China's military development that is being geared to a 'blue water' navy.

15   Ding Jie, 'Chinese Soil Experts Warn of Massive Threat to Food Security,' SciDev. net., 5 August 2010, http://www.scidev.net/en/news/chinese-soil-experts-warn-of-massive-threat-to-food-security.html.

Ongoing Tensions

If one is diligent in reading the news of the region, what can be discerned behind the façade of a supposedly united march toward 'peace and prosperity,' promised by the utopian vision of Free Trade are festering tensions throughout the Indo-Pacific. While the Big Three of the Indo-Pacific—Russia, India and China—enter into trade relationships, the disputes over territories and resources, some going back centuries are not resolved other than when China's neighbours give in to China's intransigence. It is the theme of this book that deference to China will not last indefinitely, and conflict will be ignited by one or a combination of crisis scenarios discussed herein. All of the Big Three, as it happens, continue to build-up militarily.

An article appearing on the website of the authoritative *DefenceNet* on the deployment of Russia's new Ka-52 Alligator attack helicopters shows the ancient Sino-Russian distrust has not been resolved by signing pieces of paper. The deployment sends a message to China not to take Russia for granted as lacking will, or to assume that China will be able to keep encroaching on Russia's Far East. The *DefenceNet* report reads:

> Russia shows as the main threat to China
>
> Russia for the first time in decades, since thc Soviet Union today placed newly weapon systems in Sino-Russian border area of Manchuria, demonstrating that modified Russian defence doctrine: The main threat to Russia is now officially China. Russia will put its new attack helicopters Ka-52 Alligator, and also a new high-capacity military aircraft Su-35S in the Far East.
>
> So far, the new defence systems in Russia have always been in the European part of Russia.

The two-seater helicopters of the type in production since 2008 and so far have produced 12 helicopters for testing. The tests are said to have been completed and attack helicopters began to be produced at a rate of two per month.

Also started has been the production of fighter aircraft Sukhoi Su-35S. After completing the tests the aircraft was declared '4.5 generation fighter.'[16]

India's defence modernisation is also widely seen as being directed toward China. The launching of India's first domestically constructed nuclear submarine capable of firing ballistic missiles, is part of a programme to make India a major military power in the Indo-Pacific. The INS *Arihant* is the first in its class, with four more to follow shortly. India's Chief of Naval Staff, Admiral Nirmal Verma, declared that, 'The advent of INS *Arihant* into the fleet will complete the crucial link in India's nuclear triad—the ability to fire nuclear weapons from land, air and sea.'[17] Of the missiles India's defence research organisation stated:

The Defense Research and Development Organization (DRDO) announced last month that it has successfully developed nuclear-tipped submarine-launched ballistic missiles (SLBMs). Long shrouded in secrecy, unlike surface-to-surface nuclear missiles like Agni, the SLBM was a closely-guarded secret while in development and was called the 'Sagarika Project.' In all probability, the INS Arihant will take this missile on board. So far, countries like the US, Russia, France, China and the UK have the capability to launch a submarine-based ballistic missile.[18]

---

16   DefenceNet, 24 May 2011, http://www.defencenet.gr/defence/index. php?option=com_content&task=view&id=20290&Itemid=52.

17   Sudhi Ranjan Sen, 'Why INS Arihant, Submarine in Final Stages of Testing, Is So Important,' 7 August 2012, NDTV, http://www.ndtv.com/article/india/why-ins-arihant-submarine-in-final-stages-of-testing-is-so-important-252415.

18   Ibid.

The SLBM (K-15) only has a range of 750-km. However the INS *Arihant* can also carry the 3,500-km range K-4 missile.[19]

Indian's conventional navy is, however, in a state of disrepair and obsolescence. The Indian navy has asked the Government whether it can construct submarines at a foreign shipyard,[20] that is, in Russia. Indo-Russian cooperation in defence development is of long duration.

Ranjit Pandit wrote that Russia helped with the INS *Arihant* secret nuclear reactor. The rector was 'designed, fabricated and executed in India' by Indian industry and under the direction of Indian scientists. Dr. Anil Kakodkar, Chairman of India's Atomic Energy Commission, stated of the important Russian input, 'I would also like to thank our Russian colleagues. . . . [T]hey have played a very important role as consultants, they have a lot of experience in this so their consultancy has been of great help so that I think we should acknowledge.'[21] However, Kakodkar emphasised that the reactor was of Indian design.[22]

Despite setbacks, India is pursuing a vigorous naval construction program to redress the obsolescence of much of its fleet. A *Times of India* report states:

With 46 warships and submarines being constructed, and another 49 in the pipeline under overall plans worth Rs 2.73 lakh crore, Admiral Verma said, 'Today, I am confident we do not suffer asymmetries with anyone. We

---

19   Ranjit Pandit, 'India's Elusive Nuclear Triad Will Be Operational Soon: Navy Chief,' *The Times of India*, 8 August 2012, http://articles.timesofindia.indiatimes.com/2012-08-08/india/33099651_1_ins-arihant-ssbns-slbm.

20   Ibid.

21   Pallava Bagla, 'Russians Helped With INS Arihant's Heart: Kakodkar,' NDTV, 3 August 2009, http://www.ndtv.com/article/india/russians-helped-with-ins-arihant-s-heart-kakodkar-6659?h_related_also_see.

22   Ibid.

have the wherewithal to defend our maritime interests.'[23]

There is no doubt about the reason for India's determination to add nuclear-armed submarines to their military: China, although India has been elusive when questioned on this.[24] After all, there is supposed to be a magical new entity called BRIC which places India and China together in alliance with Brazil and Russia, and is supposedly conjuring a grand new bloc between states that not only have nothing in common but which include historical enemies.

In connection with the vast current naval construction program and the INS *Arihant*, Admiral Verma has insisted that India will not deploy its naval forces in the South China Sea.[25] However, this does not accord with his franker statements in previous interviews. Suman Sharma reporting for *The Sunday Guardian*, wrote of this in 2011:

> With an eye on the strategic South China Sea, the Indian Navy is preparing to base some of its important assets on the eastern seaboard at the Vishakhapatnam-based Eastern Naval Command. It has outlined massive expansion plans for the same.

> After former President A. P. J. Abdul Kalam officially endorsed India's Look East policy in 2006, the Navy, which is considered the strategic force among the three armed forces, has been building a strong base on the eastern front.

> The Chief of Naval Staff, Admiral Nirmal Verma, on the eve of Navy Day on 4 December, Sunday, outlined an ambitious expansion plan for the service, which is eyeing a greater role in the South China Sea. Militarily,

---

23   Ranjit Pandit, op. cit.

24   Ibid.

25   Ibid.

India will have a greater footprint in the South China Sea. By 2027 the Indian Navy would have 500 aircraft, of all varieties, and 150 ships, in its inventory, with five ships every year being manufactured, after five years from now.

With Project Varsha underway, which is a special berthing base for India's indigenous SSBN INS Arihant class nuclear-powered submarines, the Naval Chief, Admiral Nirmal Verma told *The Sunday Guardian* that the first indigenous aircraft carrier too would be based in the Eastern Command. Right now the Eastern Naval Command has 45 ships and six submarines.[26]

Unsurprisingly, Admiral Verma emphasised the need for peaceful solutions for the region. China has so far achieved its ends through diplomacy and economic relations, with the occasional flash of military threat to maintain a festering intimidation in the background of the smiles and handshakes; extending its influence while appearing to compromise. Meanwhile the regional powers talk peace, but prepare for war.

Military circles in India are not fooled by China's façade of 'neighbourliness.' Recently General Vijay Kumar Singh, former Chief of Army Staff, warned that India must 'wake up' to her military shortcomings and the threat posed by China. He has stated that unresolved border disputes with China could be used as the pretext to 'put India down' at any time that China perceived India was becoming too powerful. Speaking with *The Times*, General Singh alluded to the defeat of India by China in 1962 over the disputed territory of Arunachal Pradesh, and how talks with China over the territory have entered their 32nd year without being

26 Suman Sharma, 'Navy Ready to Flex Muscles in South China Sea,' *The Sunday Guardian* (New Delhi), 4 December 2011, http://www.sunday-guardian.com/news/navy-ready-to-flex-muscles-in-south-china-sea.

resolved. He advocated increased spending on defence and talked of China's subjugation of Tibet, its wooing of Nepal and Myanmar, and its use of Pakistan as a 'cat's paw.'[27]

A recent Australian Briefing Paper on the Indo-Pacific, while commenting on Russia as being China-aligned in the Pacific region, nonetheless stated: 'But the biggest regional problem is the one Moscow leaves largely undeclared: how to regulate their vital "strategic partnership" with China, a country of which they are, inwardly, extremely wary.'[28]

INDO-RUSSIAN RELATIONS & THE US

Despite the US's best effort, India is aware of her true friends. Admiral Verma stated that regional co-operation is needed to reduce conflicts, but India continues to rebuff the US's overtures. India is aiming for the so-called 'thousand-ship concept' for the region mooted by the US, whereby there would be naval cooperation between allies in the region, with the important difference that India does not see a role for the US as part (i.e. the dominant part) of such a regional security arrangement.[29]

India has wisely been dubious about placing reliance on the US for defence purposes. In April 2011 India opted for a deal with Russia rather than US corporations, for co-development of its fifth generation fighters. The same month she rejected the prospect of upgrading strategic dialogue with the US to a joint 2 + 2 format (foreign + defence ministers). India's defence contacts with Russia, many of them in the form of co-development, account for 55% of Russia's arms exports. India has in recent years purchased

27 'Warning of Threats from China,' *The Dominion Post* (Wellington, New Zealand), 15 December 2012, B3.
28 *Roundtable Summary: Russia and the Indo-Pacific*, Australian National University's Centre for European Studies, vol. 2, no. 4, August 2012.
29 Suman Sharma, op. cit.

Russian built frigates armed with the jointly developed BrahMos supersonic cruise missiles, noted for their speed and accuracy. There is cooperation in submarine leasing and training, and over the next several years programmes for upgrading the air force.[30]

In 2012 Defense Secretary Leon E. Panetta went to India to secure military cooperation and geopolitical alignment, but was rebuffed. There was no customary joint press conference with Indian officials, and India made it plain that she would continue to pursue an independent policy. Even the enticement of arms purchases from the US did not succeed: 'India is the world's largest arms importer. Washington was disappointed last year when U.S. companies lost out on a $12-billion deal to sell 126 fighter jets to New Delhi,' states a report in the *Los Angeles Times*.

India maintains that the US offered older aircraft technology. Officials also bridle at what they see as American reluctance to transfer other sensitive technology, and Washington's insistence on after-sales, on-site inspections of equipment, part of American policy to ensure sophisticated weapons aren't diverted to rogue states.[31] Again we might see that the 'rogue states' formula serves as a catch-all for maintaining US control, and that such inspections would rather ensure that India is kept in line. India learns that with American aid and trade comes subservience to American interests.

One might get the impression that American relationships with China have long been more cordial than with India.

---

30 Dr. D. Gorenburg, Davis Center for Russian and Eurasian Studies, Harvard University, 'India-Russia Defense Integration Is Likely To Endure,' *Russian Military Reform*, 7 January 2011, http://russiamil.wordpress.com/2011/01/07/india-russia-defense-integration-is-likely-to-endure/.

31 David S. Cloud and Mark Magnier, 'India Not Sold on Closer Ties with U.S.,' *Los Angeles Times*, 6 June 2012, http://articles.latimes.com/2012/jun/06/world/la-fg-panetta-india-20120607.

Arms deals with India, 'in the pipeline,' worth $8 billion,[32] are seen as one of the few or only advances of American interests. However, as for any geopolitical alignment, such a prospect does not seem to be even on a faraway horizon, despite some news media touting of the Panetta trip and the arms deal as a great breakthrough in Indo-US relations. Indian Defense Minister A. K. Antony 'told Panetta politely but firmly that India doesn't wish to be seen as a U.S. alliance partner as it embarks on its Asia-Pacific strategy.'

> . . . [W]hile New Delhi has been open to increasing bilateral engagement with Washington—and does in fact undertake a number of joint exercises across the three defense services—the establishment in India is still wary of any military alliance, or even a formal partnership with the United States.[33]

Panetta, according to media pundits, seems to have tried to sell an alliance with the US across South East Asia on the implied basis of protection from China. The China bogeyman thus serves the US well when necessary, like the old 'Soviet menace,' but India is having none of it, or at least very little: 'Indian lawmakers and politicians continue to have reservations over the United States itself, doubts born largely from India's perception of the past half a century that Washington has tended to side with India's arch rival, Pakistan.'[34]

Defence Minister Antony has been especially careful not to publicly cosy up to Washington. Indeed, he has often instructed ministry officials to downplay joint bilateral exercises with the United States, resisted signing deals tied to weapons systems weapons, and he has consistently told

---

32 Ibid.

33 Nitin Gokhale, 'Why India Snubbed U.S.,' *The Diplomat*, 12 June 2012, http://thediplomat.com/2012/06/12/why-india-snubbed-u-s/.

34 Ibid.

officials that India believes any US disputes should be dealt with bilaterally.[35]

Despite the US playing the China card to scare small states, on the one hand, while at a higher level, pursuing a decade's long policy to integrate China as a partner in a New World Order, already manifested in the economic symbiosis between the two, India is not succumbing. While being wary of China's expansion in the region, India prefers alignment with the small states such as Vietnam.[36]

The Heritage Foundation, along with *The Wall Street Journal*, publish an index on global 'economic freedom' in which India scored 164th of 179 economies.[37] This should be *encouraging*, because it means that India still has some measure of economic sovereignty whereby the state has the option of pursuing economic planning in tandem with private enterprise, and the state bank, without interference by globalist think tanks, lobbies, transnational corporations, and international authorities such as the WTO, IMF and World Bank; all of which have brought ruin, debt, and exploitation to the world.

Hence, globalist urgings for India are that she must enter the global economy by opening up to 'free trade' (which is only really 'free' for the world oligarchy) which is the means by which the globalist economic elite dominate the economies of all states that succumb. A recent article from the US free market think tank, the Heritage Foundation, laments that India's failure to accelerate 'reform' has adversely impacted on economic relations with the US. Their advice is to 'turn away from the state' and towards the market; which is

---

35   Ibid.

36   Ibid.

37   Dr. D. Scissors, 'What Indian Economic Reform Could Mean for US,' Heritage Foundation, 18 August 2011, http://www.heritage.org/research/reports/2011/08/what-indian-economic-reform-could-mean-for-the-us.

precisely what is *not* needed. The US free marketers advise that the Indian state is 'notoriously inept.'[38] The answer, according to Dr. Scissors, is for Indian integration into the globalist economic structures: 'The potential for multilateral cooperation—at the World Trade Organization (WTO), the Asia-Pacific Economic Cooperation (APEC) Forum, and in ASEAN-centered forums—is considerable, but India's present disinterest in market reform is a major obstacle.'[39]

On the other hand, as with previous recent Indian ventures which are focused on Russia, despite US overtures, in addition to Russian consultancy for the INS *Arihant* nuclear reactor, India's ambitious naval construction program will proceed with Russian assistance. Inductions planned for 2012 included three survey vessels, one anti-submarine warfare corvette, one offshore patrol vessel, 25 fast interceptor crafts, one aircraft carrier being refitted in Russia and two *Talwar*-class destroyers from Russia.[40] Russian MiGs will fly from aircraft carriers constructed in India. The new indigenous aircraft carrier (IAC) will be based at the Indian Navy's Vishakhapatnam-based Eastern Command. As of writing, the 37,000-tonne ship is under construction at the Cochin shipyard. An additional contract for 29 Russian MiG fighters was signed in 2012.[41] However, the construction of the IACs is far behind schedule,[42] with major delays indicating that much needs to be done to construct and maintain an efficient Indian military capability for the region.

Despite historically meaningless concepts such as of 'BRIC' and the Shanghai Cooperation Organisation, Russia and

---

38   Ibid.
39   Ibid.
40   Suman Sharma, op. cit.
41   Ibid.
42   'India's Aircraft Carrier Dilemma,' 27 March 2013, http://osimint.com/2013/03/27/indias-aircraft-carrier-dilemma/.

India are just as cognisant as ever that the threat is from China. A recent joint military exercise between Russia and India was aimed surreptitiously at China, and was reported as such by Chinese and Russian analysts:

> Russia and India see China as their major rival, making the joint military exercise near Lake Baikal quite meaningful, said a Russian military analyst.
>
> Russia and India started their sixth joint anti-terrorism military exercises Indra-2012 Tuesday in the Republic of Buryatia in southern Siberia, a place near both China and Lake Baikal.
>
> 'To some extent, the exercise is targeted at China surreptitiously. At least in part of it, China is likely to be an imaginary enemy,' the military analyst said. . . .
>
> Although both Russia and India stressed the joint exercises were aimed to crack down on terrorism, the Russian analyst said it was a meaningless title . . .
>
> According to the Russian government, the drill was part of the 2011–2012 military technology cooperation program between Russia and India.[43]

CHINA'S PASSPORT MAP CONTROVERSY SYMBOLIC OF THE INTRANSIGENCE OF TERRITORIAL AMBITIONS

Buried away in the corner of a New Zealand daily newspaper, barely noticeable, was an item entitled 'China's New E-passports Cause Anger.' The meagre attention given to a major geopolitical issue is indicative of the naïve, if not outright stupid, mentalities of New Zealand journalists,

---

43 Wang Qi, 'China Acts As Imaginary Enemy in Russia-India Military Drills?,' *Sina English*, 10 August 2012, http://english.sina.com/world/2012/0809/495072.html.

politicians, diplomats, and business leaders who cannot see further than Chinese smiles, handshakes, and trade. The entire article reads as follows:

> China has redrawn the map printed in its passports to lay claim to almost all of the South China Sea, infuriating its neighbours.
>
> In the new passports, a nine dash line has been added that hugs the coasts of the Philippines, Brunei, Malaysia, Vietnam and some of Indonesia, scooping up several islands that are claimed both by China and by its neighbours.
>
> China has printed nearly six million of the passports since it quietly introduced them in April, judging by the monthly application rate.
>
> The Philippines joined Vietnam yesterday in voicing its anger at the new map.
>
> 'The Philippines strongly protests the inclusion of the nine-dash lines in the e-passport as such image covers an areas of the Philippines' territory and maritime domain,' said Albert del Rosario, a foreign affairs spokesman.[1]

This is typical of the quagmire that is called named 'Asia,' as if there is, has been, or can ever be, such a unitary bloc in geopolitical, ethnographic or even just pragmatic economic senses. 'Asia' as a unitary idea exists only in the minds of those in business, political and diplomatic circles, particularly in New Zealand, Australia and the US, who have a reductionist outlook based on trade. They are materialists who—like Marxists—believe that history is moved primarily by economic forces. Hence their solutions are legalistic,

---

1   'China's New E-passports Cause Anger,' *The Dominion Post* (Wellington, New Zealand), 24 November 2012, B3.

based on contractual law between states, such as 'free trade agreements' that can be litigated in supranational courts if a state reneges, with a final solution being military.

This surreptitious symbolic declaration of imperial expansion inaugurated by the Chinese in April 2012 was 'noticed by keen-eyed Vietnamese officials who are in the process of renewing six-month visas for Chinese businessmen,' according to the lengthier report that was carried by the London *Telegraph*.[2]

Vietnam has a long history of standing up to Chinese expansionism,[3] and was the first to challenge China on this. *The Telegraph*'s Malcolm Moore adds that 'In response, Vietnamese immigration is refusing to paste visas inside the new passports, instead putting the visa on a separate, detached, page.' Recognising the passport with a visa would imply recognition of China's claim to Vietnamese territory.[4] 'The new passport also stakes a claim to the Diaoyu or Senkakku islands, which have been a great source of friction between China and Japan.'[5]

However, *The Telegraph* report is also far from adequate, failing to even mention the very significant inclusion of the Indian territories of Arunachal Pradesh and Aksai Chin on the passport map. India in response issued visas stamped with maps of India that include Arunachal and Aksai Chin.[6] An *Indian Express* article concluded:

---

2   Malcolm Moore, 'China's neighbours protest its passport map grab,' *The Telegraph*, 22 November 2012, http://www.telegraph.co.uk/news/worldnews/asia/china/9695732/Chinas-neighbours-protest-its-passport-map-grab.html.

3   K. R. Bolton, 'Has Vietnam Lost the Struggle for Freedom?,' *Foreign Policy Journal*, 10 June 2012, http://www.foreignpolicyjournal.com/2010/06/10/has-vietnam-lost-the-struggle-for-freedom/.

4   Moore, op. cit.

5   Ibid.

6   Shubhajit Roy, 'India, China, in Passport Map Row Again,' *The Indian Express*, 24 November 2012, http://www.indianexpress.com/news/india-china-in-passport-map-row-again/1035633/.

Incidentally, the new outline map on Chinese e-passports also includes Taiwan and South China Sea in its territory, leaving Beijing's other neighbours such as the Philippines, Vietnam, Brunei and Malaysia too infuriated. Taiwan, the Philippines and Vietnam have all protested against the new map.

About three years ago, China had created a diplomatic row by issuing stapled visas to residents of Jammu and Kashmir, terming it a 'disputed territory.' It has always denied visas to those hailing from Arunachal.[7]

While India and China clashed during the 1960s over disputed territories, in 1993 and 1996 the two countries signed agreements to respect the Line of Actual Control 'to maintain peace and tranquillity.'[8] As we have seen, such agreements mean little to China and are stepping-stones towards longer-range goals. Hence the territorial agreements do not deter China from raising the matter of territorial disputes that are supposedly settled, to the extent of military incursions across India's border.

If China does not really consider the border question with India as settled, despite agreements, should Russia believe that she has settled territorial issues with China also? The disputes with Russia was supposedly settled amicably in 2008, whereby Russia handed over Yinlong Island (known as Tarabarov in Russia) and half of the Heixiazi Island (Bolshoi Ussuriysky) at the confluence of the Amur and Ussuri rivers. The agreement was thought to be the basis for a Sino-Russian rapprochement. While Russia gave up Tarabarov and half of Bolshoi Ussuriysky, totalling 174 square kilometres, China supposedly gave up its claim to

---

7   Ibid.

8   'China Shows Arunachal Pradesh and Aksai Chin as Its Territory,' *The Indian Express*, 23 November 2012, http://www.indianexpress.com/news/china-shows-arunachal-pradesh-and-aksai-chin-as-its-territory/1035332/.

the other half of Bolshoi Ussuriysky. What is noted about all these concessions is that China seems invariably to get the better end of the deal.

Russia's retreat from Central Asia with the implosion of the USSR has seen China attempt to fill the power vacuum. Indian researcher Sudha Ramachandran offered a perceptive analysis, writing of China's strategy: 'A Sino-Tajik border agreement that was ratified recently by Tajikistan's parliament flies in the face of images of China being a "bullying" and "belligerent" power that "will go to any length to fulfil its territorial ambitions."' The agreement requires Tajikistan to cede about 1,000 square kilometres of land in the Pamir Mountains to China, only 3.5% of the land China was claiming. Under border agreements with Kazakhstan and Kyrgyzstan, China received 22% and 32% respectively of disputed land. Ramachandran states that of 23 territorial disputes since 1949, China has offered 'substantial compromises' in 17, usually accepting half the territory that has been demanded.[9] Ramachandran offers an explanation for China's 'generosity' that is uncommonly insightful:

> However, there is more to it than meets the eye. The territorial concessions that China is believed to have made are not quite as substantial as they appear to be. Srikanth Kondapalli, a China expert at the Jawaharlal Nehru University in New Delhi pointed out that China's strategy of stepping up territorial claims and then settling for less has enabled it to appear to be making a major territorial concession to reach a border resolution agreement. In several disputes, 'whether China actually gave up territory or made a substantial concession is a debatable question,' he told *Asia Times Online*.

---

9   Sudha Ramachandran, 'China Plays Long Game on Border Disputes,' *Asia Times Online*, 27 January 2011, http://www.atimes.com/atimes/China/MA27Ad02.html.

. . . 'China will claim more before settling for less,' he said. 'The so-called territorial concessions that it will probably extend while settling the dispute will not merit being regarded as concessions.'[10]

Filipino diplomat Albert del Rosario, previously quoted in connection with the Chinese passport map, is cognisant of this strategy still in operation:

Lest we are lulled into a false sense of security and delude ourselves that quiet diplomacy is working, let us be wary of reports Chinese ships have withdrawn from Pag-asa in the Spratly group of islands. Remember it was Chairman Mao Zedong who said 'To take one step forward, take two steps backward.'[11]

The timing of the new passport map is a provocation that reiterates China's territorial ambitions, which warns the world that China' s diplomacy should not be taken as a sign of retreat. Shubhajit Roy writes of this timing:

Significantly, these developments occur even as a high-level team of Chinese diplomats, for the first time, visited Sikkim in connection with consular issues, which was seen as reconfirmation of Beijing's stance of accepting the state as part of India. The development comes even as Prime Minister Manmohan Singh met his Chinese counterpart Wen Jiabao on the sidelines of the Asean summit in Cambodia where the two leaders discussed ways to move forward on the vexed boundary issue.[12]

China has not compromised despite its gains, including the territorial gains achieved diplomatically with Russia. Her

---

10   Ibid.

11   Albert del Rosario, 'Two Steps Backward, One Step Forward,' *Manila Standard Today*, 1 August 2012.

12   Shubhajit Roy, op. cit.

long-range hegemonic goals remain the same. Tensions are, as paradoxical as it might appear to the naïve, increasing regardless of the superficial rapprochement of China with others in Asia and the Pacific regions. Aljazeera observes: 'Stand-offs between Chinese vessels and the Philippine and Vietnamese navies in the South China Sea have become more common as China increases patrols in waters believed to hold vast reserves of oil and natural gas.'[13] Aljazeera also observes that the dispute came at the time of an ASEAN summit: 'Malaysia and Brunei are also claimants in the dispute which overshadowed an Asian leaders' summit in Cambodia this week. China is also embroiled in a territorial dispute with Japan.'[14]

China's latest provocation is a reminder that belligerence remains, and that China's territorial demands on India will not be compromised. Such provocations seem to be aimed at reminding states that China still has a policy of territorial expansion that will be backed by military confrontation if negotiations fail. In April 2013 a Chinese platoon set up a camp 19 kilometres inside India, at Raki Nalla in north Ladakh. Negotiating for withdrawal, China insisted that India stop developing infrastructure along the Line of Actual Control. Many areas in that region remain disputed territory. A. K. Antony countered that,

it is the right of every country to develop infrastructure in their area. As China has the right to increase, improve and strengthen other facilities on its land, India has the right to develop its own infrastructure in its area. Over the years the IAF and Army have increased capability on our land and that process will continue.[15]

13   'Philippines Protest China E-passport Map,' Aljazeera, 22 November 2012, http://www.aljazeera.com/news/asia-pacific/2012/11/201211229560658870.html.

14   Aljazeera, op. cit.

15   Shigeki Nozawa, 'Islands Dispute Sparks Riots in Chinese Cities,' *Brisbane Times*, 17 September 2012, http://www.brisbanetimes.com.au/world/islands-dispute-sparks-riots-in-chinese-cities-20120916-260ge.html.

Antony used the opportunity to reiterate India's opposition to China's demands upon other states in regard to the South China Sea, where there is contention between China, Vietnam, the Philippines and Malaysia who have overlapping claims on two oil blocks in the Phu-Khanh basin of the South China Sea off the Vietnam Coast. India supports Vietnam in stating that the oil blocks are within that state's Exclusive Economic Zone;[16] another indication of future geopolitical alignments that will be considered in the final chapter.

JAPAN AND CHINA

In September 2012 the long-time antagonism between China and Japan again erupted when China sent six government vessels into the South China Sea near the disputed islands known as Senkaku in Japan and Diaoyu in China. The ships had been dispatched after Japan announced its intention of buying the islands from their private owner.[17] The Chinese response to Japanese diplomatic protests was to instigate riots against Japanese citizens and businesses in China. The *Brisbane Times* reported:

> Panasonic's factory and a Toyota dealership in the port city of Qingdao were damaged by fire, while military police were called in to control thousands demonstrating at the Japanese consulate in Shanghai as protests escalated . . . Protests occurred in Qingdao, Xi'an, Guangzhou and Hong Kong on Saturday as more than 1000 demonstrators gathered outside the Japanese embassy in Beijing. Japan's *Kyodo News* said more than

---

16   Sudhi Ranjan Sen, 'After China-Standoff, Defence Minister A. K. Antony Says India Has Right to Upgrade Infrastructure Along Border,' NDTV, 11 May 2013, http://www.ndtv.com/article/india/after-china-stand-off-defence-minister-ak-antony-says-india-has-right-to-upgrade-infrastructure-alon-365677.

17   Shigeki Nozawa, 'Islands Dispute Sparks Riots in Chinese Cities,' *Brisbane Times*, 17 September 2012, http://www.brisbanetimes.com.au/world/islands-dispute-sparks-riots-in-chinese-cities-20120916-260ge.html.

40,000 people joined demonstrations in 20 Chinese cities. . . . In Shanghai yesterday, hundreds of military police were brought in to separate groups of protesters outside the Japanese consulate, chanting: 'Down with Japan devils, boycott Japanese goods, give back Diaoyu!' There were no reports of injuries.[18]

Despite the reference to Chinese police being called in to 'control' the riots, it would be naïve to think that these demonstrations took place without the prompting of Chinese officialdom. China does not feel constrained by diplomacy or business. Chinese policy is undertaken in the pursuit of hegemonic geopolitical long-term aims that are quite beyond the comprehension of the small-minded politicians and the greed-driven enthusiasts for free trade with China. China functions on an entirely different level of reality, that of *realpolitik* and geopolitics or statecraft, something that has been missing from the West for over a century. Further, despite the calm exterior of Chinese diplomats and politicians on the world and regional stages, none of the old irrational fanaticism of the Mao era has disappeared; it can be tapped into at any time with the same crazed zeal as the Red Guards during the Mao era.

The relationship between China and Japan is complicated by the forthright refusal of Japanese businessmen and politicians to kow-tow to China for alleged atrocities during the invasion of China. This is something that rankles deeply with the Chinese, although it also serves China very well in allowing a morally indignant posture on the world stage. While Japanese Trilateralist businessmen, like their counterpart in the US, have been quick to take up business opportunities in China, unlike their American and other Western counterparts, Japanese businessmen also maintain a loyalty to their state and their Emperor that still takes precedence over profit, and which still regards business as serving the interests of the

18   Ibid.

Japanese nation, rather than in the interests of money *per se*. In other words, Japanese businessmen can be expected to be patriotic, whereas American and other Western businessmen cannot really comprehend any such 'outmoded' concepts as 'nationalism' which interferes with free trade and globalisation. China for its part has used the persistent nationalism the Japanese as a means of trying to divide Japan from its neighbours, and states that the US should focus its concerns on a possible revival of Japanese nationalism.[19]

Not only is China not compromising over territorial claims, it is extending them. China now claims Okinawa, in addition to the Senkakus island chain in the East China Sea controlled by Japan. In May 2013 China broached the matter of Okinawa with an article by two academics in the official newspaper, *The People's Daily*. In fact, the article advocated Chinese sovereignty over the island chain of Ryukyu, of which Okinawa is a part. The claim to the Ryukyus is justified, according to Luo Yuan, a two-star general in the People's Liberation Army, by stating that the island started paying tribute to China in 1372. Li Guoqiang and Zhang Haipeng, of the Chinese Academy of Social Sciences stated in their *People's Daily* article that the 'unresolved' question of the Ryukyus should now be open for 'reconsideration.' In reply to Japanese protests, Hua Chunying, a spokeswoman for the foreign ministry, said that China 'does not accept Japan's representations or protests.'[20] The reaction of China to Japanese concerns, as with India, is one of contemptuous indifference.

At the time of the anti-Japanese rioting in China over the disputed Senkakus US Defense Secretary Leon Panetta was in China 'reassuring Chinese leaders the Obama administration's

19   Michelle Flor Cruz, 'US Takes Japan's Side on Disputed Territory in East China Sea,' *International Business Times*, 3 May 2013, http://www.ibtimes.com/us-takes-japans-side-disputed-territory-east-china-sea-saying-senkaku-islands-fall-under-security.

20   Justin McCurry, 'Japan Lays Claim to Okinawa as Territory Dispute with Japan Escalates,' *The Guardian*, 15 May 2013.

pivot to Asia is not meant to provoke a confrontation over China's increasingly assertive posture towards its neighbours.'[21] Was this a warning to Japan and others that, despite the rhetoric on the world and regional stages, the US interest in the Indo-Pacific does not include a policy of containing China? Although US Defense Secretary Chuck Hagel met with his Japanese counterpart Itsunori Onodera in May 2013 and gave Japan assurances of US support for control of the islands, given that US troops are stationed on Okinawa, how far would the US react to Chinese provocations against Japan?

While the US and China extend into the Pacific, Putin's Russia has a new agenda in the region. Putin stated at the APEC summit held in 1912 that Russia is an 'intrinsic part of the Asia Pacific region.' However, Russia will have to contend with both the US and China. The APEC meeting was held in Vladivostok, whose name means 'Lord of the East,' named after China ceded the territory to Russia in 1860.[22] The symbolism of the Vladivostok summit would not have been lost on China. Was this the reason why China flexed her muscles several weeks later in regard to Japanese sovereignty over the Senkaku islands, reminding Russia that she has been a declining power, while China has been in the ascent? Further realistic thinking came from a RAND analyst:

> 'There are those in Russia who see China as a prospective threat' despite the two countries' close relationship, said Olga Oliker, senior international policy analyst at the RAND Corporation. 'If Russia does find a way to greater prominence in Asia, it is possible that Russia will find its own interests and pursue them, not always in ways that align with China's needs.'[23]

---

21 Nozawa, 'Islands Dispute Sparks Riots in Chinese Cities.'

22 'Putin's Pacific Ambitions Face Challenge,' gulfnews.com, 10 September 2012, http://gulfnews.com/news/world/other-world/putin-s-pacific-ambitions-face-challenge-1.1072562.

23 Ibid.

Regional Globalisation[24]

The Trans-Pacific Partnership (TPP) is an important part of the globalisation process that has been decades in the making. The process was formalised on 12 November 2011. While a 'Pacific community' similar to the 'European Community' has often been mooted by New Zealand and Australian politicians,[25] the TPP creates the foundation for full-fledged regional governance. Presently the states that comprise this TPP include Australia, Brunei Darussalam, Chile, Malaysia, New Zealand, Peru, Singapore, Vietnam, and the United States.[26]

The current format of this regional pact was announced by Ambassador Ron Kirk to the US Congress on 14 December 2009. As a free trade regional agreement, this means that each state will be obliged to open itself up to imports and a regional economic rationalisation process that will ruthlessly eliminate those national industries that cannot compete. It means that once in, like other free trade agreements, extricating oneself becomes impossible. The much lauded prospects of increased employment and economic opportunities, by which such agreements are sold, such as that entered into by New Zealand with China does not—obviously—eventuate. 'Partnership' and 'competitiveness'[27] are used simultaneously, yet free trade intrinsically does not include 'partnership'; it means driving the 'weaker' to the wall on the pretext that the best survive and thereby the general economy is strengthened. It takes no account of national requirements, strategic needs, and

---

24 This paper was originally published by *Foreign Policy Journal*, 19 November 2011.

25 For example, former New Zealand Labour Minister Mike Moore is a long time enthusiast for a 'Pacific community' and was rewarded for his conversion from 'socialism' to free trade by being made head of the World Trade Organization. His globalist credentials include membership of the Trilateral Commission.

26 'Trans-Pacific Partnership,' Office of the US Trade Representative, http://www. ustr.gov/tpp.

27 'Outlines of the Trans-Pacific Partnership,' ibid.

ties each state to the rise or fall of the major players in a gamble with entire nations.

When Kevin Rudd became Australian Prime Minister in 2008, he floated ideas for a Pacific regional bloc that are close to what is transpiring with the TPP. What is significant, in identifying the globalist interests that are promoting this agenda, is that Rudd presented the idea to his countrymen via a speech to the Australian branch of the Asia Society, which will be considered below. In the speech he went beyond the usual call for a closer regional agreement between Australia, New Zealand, and the South Pacific island nations, and advocated its broadening to include the US and China. That is to say, the Pacific community idea which in many ways is desirable; especially if it could *minimise* the influence of China and the US in the region, has been broadened to being exactly what was always intended: a step toward globalisation at the behest of US-based plutocracy. What Rudd said a few years ago is instructive in providing background for the present TPP, which focuses on the US and is broadened to Pacific Rim South American states.

Nonsense about each state doing what one can do best has been used for several decades now to sell the idea of economic rationalisation. Any state that embarks on such a course of revived 19th-century economics is left with a ravaged economy that has no chance of being self-supporting. Economic rationalisation in the name of 'efficiency' creates a permanent pool of the unemployable because the champions of free market economics believe, as economic reductionists, that humans are interchangeable economic units that are infinitely malleable and can fit into whatever new environment is contrived. When the theory does not accord with reality, the victims, the new pool of unemployed, are further victimised as 'welfare parasites.' Free Trade, and its method of economic rationalisation, is a failed dogma. New Zealand began the process of rationalisation decades ago by the start of a long process of opening up to imports, on the assumption that 'inefficient' businesses would fall, and leave only the best and most suitable to fit into a regional and ultimately a world economy (the 'New International Economic Order' as it was then called). The result was the destruction of New Zealand manufacturing, which has resulted in a large pool of unemployables, because the politicians cannot or will not understand that not everyone of working age is capable of being an IT worker. New Zealand's labour intensive economy was wrecked for the sake of a globalist agenda and we today see the consequences.

The great achievement that has been negotiated is therefore to extend failed economic dogma beyond national levels and to the regional, in order that a very small element of business can expand without national impediments.

Globalist interests in the US have not been pushing this 'economic integration' as a humanitarian gesture. It is an important exercise in international power-politics. The other member states will be prostrate before the US plutocracy as their resources come under the domination of free trade investment clauses in the TPP agreement. TPP will be sold in the other states as a great opportunity to sell exports to a big market. This is nonsense. We have seen how the Free Trade Agreement between China and New Zealand operates. Under Free Trade, the big dominates and often eliminate the little. The US administration is selling TPP with *national* rather than globalist rhetoric: 'Increasing American Exports, Supporting American Jobs.'[1] Under Free Trade, there are winners and losers, and even recourse to war when the losers are no longer sustainable and fight rather than roll over and die, or when one export power

---

1 'The United States in the Trans-Pacific Partnership,' http://www.ustr.gov/about-us/press-office/fact-sheets/2011/november/united-states-trans-pacific-partnership.

conflicts with the interests of another, as in the case of World War II resulting from the success of German trade expansion in Europe and its extension into South American markets.

Free Trade has been imposed upon the world as the economic foundation for a US-dominated order since Woodrow Wilson's 'Fourteen Points.' The policy was reiterated by Roosevelt in the 'Atlantic Charter.' The rhetoric has not changed for decades. When Roosevelt was laying down the terms for the post-war world to Churchill, he stated:

> Of course, after the war, one of the preconditions of any lasting peace will have to be the greatest possible freedom of trade. No artificial barriers. As few favoured economic agreements as possible. Opportunities for expansion. Markets open for healthy competition.[2]

> . . . Will anyone suggest that Germany's attempt to dominate trade in central Europe was not a major contributing factor to war?[3]

International trade brings war, not peace, as it is a façade for domination by hegemonic interests. The terms of the TPP are intended to benefit the US, which means US-based globalist plutocrats, the Office of the US Trade Representative stating:

> Cross-cutting issues not previously in trade agreements, such as making the regulatory systems of TPP countries more compatible so U.S. companies can operate more seamlessly in TPP markets, and helping innovative, job-creating small-and medium-sized enterprises participate more actively in international trade.[4]

---

2   Elliott Roosevelt, *As He Saw It* (New York: Duell, Sloan and Pearce, 1946), 35.

3   Ibid.

4   'The United States in the Trans-Pacific Partnership.'

Economic structures are therefore to be rationalised regionally to permit free entry for US encroachments. Reference to the benefits for small- and medium-sized enterprises is nonsense, as rationalisation drives such enterprises to the wall. No state will be able to protect such enterprises, as it will be regarded as interfering in the free market and as unfair competition. State-owned enterprises are also to be subjected to competition from the globalist corporations. As it is, many of the states involved have been selling their state assets and enterprises, generally to make interest payments on debts to international finance. What is left of state assets will be taken over by the major corporations, and national governments, such as they remain, will not be able to interfere because of regional regulations imposed by the TPP and enforced by TPP laws and bureaucracies. Note that the above passage from the TPP principles states that regulations of each state will be altered to make national economies compatible with US corporate interests. The TPP's terms will ensure that 'state-owned enterprises compete fairly with private companies and do not distort competition in ways that put U.S. companies and workers at a disadvantage.'[5] This means pitting the state against private business in the free market, although state assets should be regarded as being of a strategic and not strictly an economic character. However, under Free Trade there is no such concept as a 'strategic national interest.'

The nine founding states of the TPP are intended as the beginning of a wider process, 'and will begin bilateral processes with these interested countries to discuss their readiness and ambition to meet the standards and objectives of the TPP.'[6]

The ramifications of the TPP will be known only as they take

---

5   Ibid.
6   Ibid.

effect as—apart from the final declaration—the documents of the agreement are to be kept secret for four years from ratification.[7]

GLOBALISTS' PACIFIC AGENDA

What Kevin Rudd proposed in 2008 was the agenda of the Trilateral Commission, created in 1973 by David Rockefeller. The Trilateral Commission was established as a think tank of globalist political and business leaders incorporating the US, Europe and Japan. What is notable in the context of the TPP is that the Trilateral Commission (TC) a few years ago extended its agenda to include Mexico, and the 'Japan Group' has now become the 'Pacific Asian Group.' Japan has stated its interest in joining the TPP.[8] Although Mexico is not one of the founding member states of the TPP, the extension of Trilateralism, which originally focused on North America, Europe and Japan, was extended to Latin America and to Asia as a whole. The TC stated of this:

> Two strong convictions guide our thinking for the 2006–2009 triennium. First, the Trilateral Commission remains as important as ever in helping our countries fulfil their shared leadership responsibilities in the wider international system and, second, its framework needs to be widened to reflect broader changes in the world. Thus, the Japan Group has become a Pacific Asian Group, and Mexican members have been added to the North American Group. The European Group continues to widen in line with the enlargement of the EU.[9]

7   TPP Watch, http://tppwatch.org/2011/10/16/trans-pacific-partnership-papers-remain-secret-for-four-years-after-deal/.

8   K. Kim, 'Obama: Outlines of TransPacific Partnership Reached,' *Global Post*, 14 November 2011, http://www.globalpost.com/dispatch/news/regions/americas/united-states/111114/obama-outlines-transpacific-partnership-trade-de.

9   The Trilateral Commission, 'About the Organization,' http://www.trilateral.org/

Of the TC Pacific Asian Group, members are drawn from the following countries to reflect this aim of a Pacific-wide union: In 2000, the Japanese group of 85 members expanded to become a Pacific Asian group of 96 members, and includes 57 members from Japan, 15 members from Korea, 8 from Australia and New Zealand, 16 from the original five ASEAN countries (Indonesia, Malaysia, the Philippines, Singapore and Thailand). The new Pacific Asian group also includes participants from the People's Republic of China, Hong Kong and Taiwan.[10]

The Commission also implies that these regional groupings are the prelude to a 'new world order':

> The 'growing interdependence' that so impressed the founders of the Trilateral Commission in the early 1970s is deepening into 'globalisation.' The need for shared thinking and leadership by the Trilateral countries, who (along with the principal international organizations) remain the primary anchors of the wider international system, has not diminished but, if anything, intensified. At the same time, their leadership must change to take into account the dramatic transformation of the international system. As relations with other countries become more mature—and power more diffuse—the leadership tasks of the original Trilateral countries need to be carried out with others to an increasing extent.[11]

This process of 'interdependence' growing into 'globalisation' and a 'dramatic transformation of the international system' has been deliberately pushed by the Trilateral Commission, and similar bodies such as the Bilderberg Group and the Council on Foreign Relations, all of which have significant interlocking memberships.

---

about.htm.

10 Ibid.

11 Ibid.

It is not part of some organic historical process; it is a contrivance. The Trilateralist statement above alludes to the broadening of the Trilateralist countries to 'others'; again in this instance not just Japan, but the entirety of Asia and the Pacific. Although Trilateralists have dominated the Japanese business and political Establishments, they were hitherto restrained from entering into globalist agreements by the strength of the farming sector that feared American agricultural imports. The globalists have already stated that TPP means little until Japan is incorporated into it:

> But if the TPP were to remain as it is presently constituted—without Japan's inclusion—the agreement would not be the economic boon many hoped it would. . . . U.S. Deputy Secretary of State William Burns said in Tokyo in October that the United States would 'welcome Japan's interest in the TPP, recognizing of course that Japan's decision to pursue joining will be made based on its own careful considerations of its priorities and interests.' For its part, Tokyo seems ready to join the talks. Japanese entry has been on the table since October 2010, when then Prime Minister Naoto Kan and his foreign minister, Seiji Maehara, both endorsed it.[12]

However, as with other such regionalist groupings, such as the European Union, the catalyst is recognition of an outer threat; in this case, China, which has recently acted in typically belligerent and overbearing manner towards Japan over disputed territorial claims.[13] It was a similar threat supposedly posed by the USSR that drove Europe into a 'union' under American auspices and on US terms. Just what type of protection from Chinese intransigence would be accorded by the TPP under US Big Brother is

---

12   B. K. Gordon, 'The Trans-Pacific Partnership and the Rise of China: What Japan Joining the TPP Means for the Region,' Council on Foreign Relations, *Foreign Affairs*, 7 November 2011, http://www.foreignaffairs.com/articles/136647/bernard-k-gordon/the-trans-pacific-partnership-and-the-rise-of-china.

13   Ibid.

indicated by the close relationship that has long existed between China and the same globalists who have been promoting the Pacific union concept. China is represented on the boards of bodies such as the TC and the Pacific Basin Economic Council, another long-running lobby that aims for 'economic integration.' New Zealand's FTA with China is pivotal to the village idiot vision of New Zealand's economy, and any involvement with TPP is going to have to recognise China as a regional power in partnership with the US, and not as a rival power in the region. Indeed, Henry Kissinger, like George Soros, regards China as the logical partner with the US in reshaping the world, or more specifically in Kissinger's projections, a Pacific region economy. In the last chapter of his new book, Kissinger calls for a 'Pacific community' that includes China and India. Kissinger states outright that this regional bloc should be run as a *joint venture between the US and China*. Kissinger's position is summarised in a review of his book *On China* in *The Washington Post*:

> While both governments officially emphasize cooperation, he addresses the question of an inevitable clash. Will the approaching reality of economic parity overwhelm good intentions? Essentially, Kissinger's answer is no, because parity is not equality. As China's economy nears the size of America's, its per-capita income will still be one-quarter of ours, and its work force will have entered a rapid decline to old age. China's demographic constraints will limit its future growth and increase its welfare burden. Rather than preparing for a showdown with China, Kissinger suggests building a Pacific Community along the lines of the Atlantic Community to promote security through inclusivity and mutual respect.[14]

---

14   Brantly Womack, 'Henry Kissinger's "On China,"' *The Washington Post*, 4 June 2011, http://www.washingtonpost.com/entertainment/books/henry-kissingers-on-china/2011/05/17/AGE7OLIH_story.htm.

Two dominating powers within the region—China and the US—do not imply 'inclusively and mutual respect'; they imply bipolar domination. Kissinger is correct in pointing to the problems facing China's economy, but the problems facing the US give no room for optimism, as with burgeoning debt and welfare and the dismantling of American manufacturing in the quest for global economic rationalisation. The globalists hope that these two edifices will mutually prop each other up, as rivalry would be suicidal, given, for example, the rise of India, the suspicions regarding China, throughout the Indo-Pacific and the persistent wariness of Russia in regard to China. From the perspective of the globalists, of which Kissinger is both a veteran ideologue and an old China hand, a Sino-American axis makes more sense than confrontation.

The ratification of the TPP in 2011 placed the statements made by Australian Prime Minister Kevin Rudd in context, especially in regard to his having delivered the speech before the Asia Society, a long-running Rockefeller think tank that predates the Trilateral Commission. Media reports at the time stated:

Prime Minister Kevin Rudd has called on Asian and Pacific nations to form a regional alliance similar to the European Union. Mr. Rudd says a strong multilateral body is needed to help the region maintain security, foster trade and respond to natural disasters and terrorism. He said Asia needs to react quickly to cope with changes brought about by rapid economic growth in the region.

'The European Union does not represent an identikit model of what we would seek to develop in the Asia-Pacific, but what we can learn from Europe is this—it is necessary to take the first step,' he said. But he concedes getting Asian nations together will be much tougher than the task faced by the architects of the European Union last century.

'Our special challenge is that we face a region with a greater diversity in political systems and economic structures, levels of development, religious beliefs, languages and cultures than our counterparts in Europe,' he said. 'But that should not stop us from thinking big.' The Government will appoint experienced diplomat Richard Woolcott as an envoy to discuss Mr. Rudd's idea with other countries.

Mr. Rudd says the institution should span the entire Asian-Pacific region including the United States, Japan, China, India and Indonesia. 'The danger in not acting is that we run the risk of succumbing to the perception that future conflict in our region may somehow be inevitable,' he said. Mr. Rudd will use his visit to Japan and Indonesia next week to lobby Asian nations on the proposal.[15]

Rudd's speech was delivered to the Asia Society's Australian branch, called Austral Asia Center, in Melbourne. Note that Australia is referred to as 'Austral Asia' by the Society, a play on words of a term normally used to describe Australia and New Zealand. This reflects how the global plutocrats see the nations of Australia and New Zealand, and politicians such as New Zealand's former Prime Minister Jim Bolger have long referred to New Zealand as an 'Asian country.' The 'Austral Asian' branch was founded by veteran diplomat Richard Woolcott who was chosen by Rudd to initiate the 'Asia Pacific community' with high-level meetings throughout Asia, as noted in the news media

---

15   Rudd speaking to the Asia Society Austral Asia Centre, 6 June 2008; reported in *The Australian*, 7 June 2008, et al. See the report on Rudd at the Asia Society Australasia Centre's website: http://www.asiasociety.org.au/speeches/speeches_current/r155_PM_Rudd_AD2008.html.

reports. Hence, the groundwork was further laid for TPP in 2008.

The head office of the Asia Center in New York states that the Society was founded in 1956 by John D. Rockefeller III.[16] Trustees include: Charles P. Rockefeller and John D. Rockefeller IV. The 50th anniversary of the Asia Society in 2006 was a tribute to the 'whole Rockefeller family' and its vision for Asia. The 'keynote addresses' were given by Henry Kissinger, the perennial and ubiquitous government adviser; David Rockefeller,[17] head of the globalist dynasty; John D. Rockefeller IV; Charles Percy Rockefeller; and Arthur Ross, a scholar and diplomat of varied experience, who sat on the Rockefeller University Council. The by-line on the Asia Society's website is: 'Preparing Asians and Americans for a shared future.' The 'shared future' is that of unrestrained plutocracy, sold with sweeteners, maintained with debt, and enforced with bombs.

---

16 Asia Society, 'About,' http://www.asiasociety.org/about/mission.html.

17 In the course of his address David Rockefeller referred to Kissinger as his 'dear friend' and Asia Society Chairman Richard Holbrooke as his 'old friend.'

Towards an ANZAC-Indo-Russian Alliance?

Since the implosion of the Soviet bloc, a 'unipolar' world has emerged around the US. The US manipulates Islam to vigorously pursue its world policies in the name of 'the war on terrorism,' this being the guise by which President George H. W. Bush announced the intention of leading the United Nations into a 'new world order.' Islam has taken over from the 'Soviet menace' as the 'world bogeyman.' Russia and China pose as allies in confronting this unipolar post-Cold War situation by forming a pact between each other and bordering states, the Central Asia and Shanghai Cooperation Organisation. This holds out the prospect of a Eurasian bloc to confront the world hegemony of the US, which seeks to draw to it the European Union and return Europe to the subordinate role she played vis-à-vis the US during the Cold War, pushed into coming under the US orbit by the fear of Warsaw Pact invasion. It is by no means clear that the US has a long-range commitment to containing China. However, the economies of China and the US are symbiotic and both share a wariness of Russia.

There has for decades existed a pro-China lobby, including some of the US's leading political and business figures, one of whose public manifestations is the Trilateral Commission created by David Rockefeller. These 'Trilateralists,' et al. see the creation of regional blocs as the prelude to a 'new world order,' and one such bloc is envisaged as being that of an Asian economic community along similar lines to that of the European Union. China's expanding economic, military, and diplomatic influence, and India's recent emergence as a rival power, have wide geopolitical implications involving Russia. Between these powers and the possibility of military confrontation over water resources, the traditionally 'Western' societies of Australia and New Zealand have placed their futures in a China-dominated Asian bloc in the belief that their export-driven economies can only thrive in such a vast market.

The alternative presented here is between globalist regionalisation and geopolitical vectors.

The Australia-New Zealand relationship with the US stems from the generally perceived, although incorrect, perception that the Americans saved New Zealand and Australian from Japanese domination during World War II. Secondly, the US displaced Britain in the aftermath of World War II, when Britain, exhausted and indebted, scuttled her Empire, with an irresistible push from the US, and more recently when Britain joined the European Economic Community and stopped being New Zealand's and Australia's primary trading partner. Asia and especially China, and the US have filled the void. Australia and New Zealand seek to straddle both China and the US simultaneously. However trading relationships with India and Russia are also developing recently. Misplaced loyalty to the US has prevented a realistic perception of New Zealand's and Australia's place in the Indo-Pacific especially in regard to matters of defence and security.

ANZAC[18] FAITH IN US ALLIANCE MISPLACED

New Zealanders, particularly of the World War II and Korean and Vietnam War generations, have maintained a dogmatic faith in the US as an unshakable friend. If this supposedly eternal American friendship is questioned, it is regarded as being from those who were 'too young to remember the war' and the fear of a Japanese invasion. However Australian Cabinet papers have been released that confirm there was no US guarantee of military protection under the ANZUS alliance, and that the Muldoon Government sought to deceive New Zealanders into maintaining the great myth of the American protective umbrella.

---

18   ANZAC is the acronym of Australia New Zealand Army Corps, the joint military expedition at Gallipoli during World War I, which is a founding mythos of nationhood for both, and now generally refers to the historically close relationship between the two.

The foundations of New Zealand's post-war eternal gratitude and moral basis for alliances with the US rest on the myth of America supposedly defending New Zealand from an imminent Japanese invasion during World War II. It remains common for any criticism of US-NZ relations to be met with an indignant retort that America 'saved us.'

What should be sufficiently well-known, at least among informed Americans, was the determination of President Roosevelt to get the US into a war against the Axis on some pretext that, like '9/11,' would give the US an unassailable moral high-ground. The US ultimatum to Japan and the blockade are tactics now well-known on the world stage and are often a prelude to American military attack. In 1967 Colonel Curtis B. Dall, who had been President Franklin D. Roosevelt's son-in-law and who witnessed the Machiavellian machinations of the President and entourage, visited Admiral Husband E. Kimmel, who had been commander of the US Fleet at Pearl Harbor at the time of the Japanese attack. Kimmel related to Dall that,

> I found out later that the Japanese Task Force approaching Pearl Harbor had specific orders that if the American Forces at Pearl Harbor became alerted, before the attack was launched, their Task Force was to return at once to Japanese waters, without attack! Hence, to me this explained why much vitally important information in the decoded and translated Japanese cables received from Washington was deliberately withheld from the U.S. Commanders at Hawaii, lest the Japs alter their plans to attack under favourable conditions duly created for them by Washington.[19]

It is assumed that Japan aimed for an empire that encompassed the whole of Asia and the Pacific reaching down to Australia and New Zealand. This is as mythical

---

19   Curtis B. Dall, *FDR: My Exploited Father-in-Law* (Tulsa, OK: Christian Crusade Publications, 1968), 162.

as the supposition that Germany wanted to 'rule the world.' Japan, like Germany and Italy, but unlike the US, had limited aims insofar as these three primary Axis states sought sufficient living space and raw materials to achieve autarchic geopolitical blocs. In the case of Japan, their projected 'Co-Prosperity Sphere' did *not* include Australia and New Zealand. Robert W. Coakley in an official history of the US Army writes of this:

> Japan entered World War II with limited aims and with the intention of fighting a limited war. Its principal objectives were to secure the resources of Southeast Asia and much of China and to establish a 'Greater East Asia Co-Prosperity Sphere' under Japanese hegemony. In 1895 and in 1905 Japan had gained important objectives without completely defeating China or Russia and in 1941 Japan sought to achieve its hegemony over East Asia in similar fashion.[20]

Coakley, however, accepts the orthodox view of Pearl Harbor, writing of this:

> . . . The operational strategy the Japanese adopted to start war, however, doomed their hopes of limiting the conflict. Japan believed it necessary to destroy or neutralize American striking power in the Pacific the U.S. Pacific Fleet at Pearl Harbor and the U.S. Far East Air Force in the Philippines . . . Japan thought that the Allies would wear themselves out in fruitless frontal assaults against the perimeter and would ultimately settle for a negotiated peace that would leave it in possession of most of its conquests.

> . . . The Japanese were remarkably successful in the

---

20   R. W. Coakley, 'World War II: The War Against Japan,' *American Military History* (Army Historical Series, Office of the Chief of Military History, US Army), Chapter 23, 501.

execution of their offensive plan and by early 1942 had reached their intended perimeter. But they miscalculated the effect of their surprise attack at Pearl Harbor which unified a divided people and aroused the United States to wage a total, not a limited, war. As a result Japan lost, in the long run, any chance of conducting the war on its own terms. The Allies, responding to their defeats, sought no negotiated peace, but immediately began to seek means to strike back.[21]

If certain European imperial interests would be threatened by the Japanese in that region, then the outcome of the war showed that the US threat to those interests was no less determined, albeit more subtle, and therefore more treacherous. The war effectively ended the European empires, and paved the way for unlimited US global hegemony. A by-product has been the detaching of Australia and New Zealand from Britain and the Commonwealth. This destruction of the traditional concept of 'empire,' of those of America's wartime European allies, just as much as the new but short-lived empires of the Axis, for the purpose of creating a post-war world order under the domination of largely US-based international capital—not hindered by 'imperial preferences' in trade—was the primary war aim of American's ruling cabal. For the sake of vanity, Churchill wrecked the Empire he wished to defend, and realised too late that the US had no intention of letting the pre-War imperial *status quo* endure. Free Trade has been imposed upon the world as the economic foundation for a US-dominated global order since Woodrow Wilson's 'Fourteen Points.' The foundations of the post-war world laid out in the 'Atlantic Charter' rested on US-dominated Free Trade on the ruins of any concept of empire, which is to say, autarchic trading blocs. When Roosevelt was laying down the terms for the post-war world to Churchill, he stated:

---

21   Ibid., 502.

Of course, after the war, one of the preconditions of any lasting peace will have to be the greatest possible freedom of trade. No artificial barriers. As few favoured economic agreements as possible. Opportunities for expansion. Markets open for healthy competition. . . . Will anyone suggest that Germany's attempt to dominate trade in central Europe was not a major contributing factor to war?[22]

Concomitant with trade was also the question of international finance. The Axis states had withdrawn from the international trading and banking system, and created state credit[23] which generated prosperity in the midst of a world depression.[24] There was nothing intrinsically totalitarian about their methods in this sphere. They were much the same as those enacted by New Zealand[25] and Canada[26] in issuing state credit, at about the same period. Again, in the realm of international finance the edifice erected in the aftermath of World War II, that of the Bretton

---

22 Elliott Roosevelt, *As He Saw It* (New York: Duell, Sloan and Pearce, 1946), 35.

23 Henry C. K. Liu, 'Nazism and the German Economic Miracle,' *Asia Times Online*, 24 May 2005, http://www.atimes.com/atimes/Global_Economy/GE24Dj01.html.

24 The works of Social Credit founder C. H. Douglas were particularly popular in pre-war Japan, and he had visited there in 1929 as part of an engineers' conference where he delivered a paper. The Imperial House had been the major stockholder of the Bank of Japan since 1882, but in 1932 the bank was reorganised as a specifically state bank. By 1942 the reform of Japanese banking was complete, with the Bank of Japan Law modelled after the Reichsbank Act of Germany, 1939. Japan during the Depression era, like Germany, was notably prosperous through these measures. See: K. R. Bolton, *The Banking Swindle: Money Creation and the State* (London: Black House Publishing, 2013), 116–17.

25 The New Zealand Labour Government in 1936 nationalised the Reserve Bank, and issued state credit at 1% interest, to fund the iconic state housing programme, which alone reduced unemployment by 75%. Cedric Firth and Gordon Wilson, *State Housing in New Zealand* (Wellington: Government Printing Office, 1949), Bolton, *The Banking Swindle*, 96–100.

26 Harold Chorney, Associate Professor of Political Economy and Public Policy, Concordia University, Montreal; John Hotson, Professor of Economics, University of Waterloo; Mario Seccareccia, Associate Professor of Economics, University of Ottawa; The Deficit Made Me Do It!, 'Introduction,' CCPA Popular Economics Series, Editor: Ed Finn, Canadian Centre For Policy Alternatives, 2010, http://lists.topica.com/lists/VOW/read/message.html?mid=813781210&sort=d&start=6327. Also, Bolton, *The Banking Swindle*, 101–2.

Woods system, was designed to secure the global hegemony of international banking interests; a system based on compound debt, the consequences of which have finally and unequivocally caught up with much of the world in today's international 'debt crisis.'[27] That India has escaped this crisis is accounted for by her continuation of banking policies that are still overseen by the state, while other nations long ago adopted a 'hands-off' policy of the state in the crucial area of banking.

With the defeat of the Axis and the rejection by Stalin of the US's proffered 'new world order.' The myth of the Russian menace became the post-war pretext for globe-spanning US 'protection' from its former Soviet ally. The result was the 'Cold War.'[28] The US, having just made great sacrifices to 'save the world from Fascism,' quickly raised its hand to become the world policeman to 'save the world from Communism.' The result was NATO, SEATO and ANZUS. The US has ever since been looked upon as Big Brother, especially by New Zealanders and Australians ever-thankful for the kindness of the US in saving them from Japan.

New Zealanders and Australians remain blissfully unaware as to just how unreliable the US is as an ally to 'save' us from anything other than when US global interests are at stake. New Zealanders and Australians are naïve to continue thinking, despite its nefarious actions since 1945, that the US will jump to their defence if threatened by anyone. Again this blind faith is predicated on the US war against Japan, and on the assumption that the US fulfils the role that Britain once fulfilled as protector. This post-war friendship was based on alliances with the

---

27   Bolton, *The Banking Swindle*, inter alia.

28   K. R. Bolton, 'Origins of the Cold War and How Stalin Foiled a New World Order,' *Foreign Policy Journal*, 31 May 2010, http://www.foreignpolicyjournal.com/2010/05/31/origins-of-the-cold-war-how-stalin-foild-a-new-world-order.

assumption that these meant that should Australia and/or New Zealand be attacked then they were guaranteed US military intervention. New Zealanders fought in Vietnam under such assumptions and has provided troops to serve US global interests in Serbia, Afghanistan and many other states that have been subjugated by our American friends on the pretext of fulfilling United Nations 'peacekeeping' roles.

Recently released 1983 Australian Cabinet papers dispel these myths about the US, and the dishonesty of New Zealand politicians in maintaining the myth: 'The Government of the late Sir Robert Muldoon tried to persuade the United States to mislead New Zealanders on the extent of its commitment to defend the country under the Anzus alliance, confidential Australian papers reveal.'[29]

The papers show that the National Government, which was fawningly pro-US and anti-Soviet, was fearful that faith in the American alliance would be diminished if the public understood that there were no US guarantees of military intervention in the event of a military threat. 'And while the then Secretary of State, George Shultz, had explained those limits "quite categorically" during talks between alliance ministers, both the US and New Zealand fudged the reality of America's position in the communiqué the Anzus Council issued.'

While the Labour Government's *de facto* ban on US warships ended America's commitment under ANZUS, US-Australia relations were maintained but the Australian Government was under no illusions as to the extent of US guarantees. The wording of the 1952 ANZUS Treaty and

---

29   Greg Ansley, 'Muldoon Tried to Get US to Mislead NZ Public,' *The New Zealand Herald* (Auckland), 2 January 2012, http://www.nzherald.co.nz/nz/news/article. cfm?c_id=1&objectid=10776287.

President Nixon's 1969 'Guam Doctrine'[30] stated that US military intervention could not be assumed. Secretary of State Dean Acheson had stated as early as 1950 that the US's military guarantees in the Pacific region were very limited.[31] The 1983 ANZUS Council declaration from Washington sought to obscure the limitations of the alliance. The Australian Cabinet papers show that 'Australia and New Zealand could expect the US to "assist" in circumstances of a great power conflict, but that this could not be taken for granted in a lesser contingency involving the use of force.'[32] Similarly, that year Dr. Desmond Ball of Australian National University, warned New Zealand that military assistance from the US 'would depend on the specific identity of the "national adversary and the relationship of the US to the aggressor."'[33]

In 1982, at the time of the US's *de facto* alliance with China against the USSR, US National Security adviser William Clark reiterated to Australian Prime Minister Malcolm Fraser that the US's allies 'would be expected to cope alone with any local or regional conflict. If there was a conflict with a regional power, and it was just that, well, maybe that is a matter where we would be expected to look after ourselves,' Malcolm Fraser stated, unless threat power was backed by the USSR.[34]

What the history of relations between the US and Australasia show is that far from America being a steadfast friend of Australia and New Zealand, who 'saved' us from

---

30 J. L. S. Girling, 'The Guam Doctrine,' *International Affairs*, Royal Institute of International Affairs, vol. 46, no. 1, January 1970 (Blackwell Publishing), 48–62, passim.

31 Dean Acheson, 12 January 1950, cited by Girling, 'The Guam Doctrine,' 48.

32 Ansley, 'Muldoon Tried to Get US to Mislead NZ Public.'

33 *The Evening Post* (Wellington, New Zealand), 3 May 1983. Currently Dr. Ball is Professor, Strategic & Defence Studies Centre, School of International, Political & Strategic Studies, ANU.

34 *The Dominion* (Wellington, New Zealand), 29 May 1982.

the Japanese, Vietcong and Russians because of their generous outlook, the US has proceeded with its own egocentric interests. New Zealanders and Australians owe the US nothing, and the sentimental attachment many New Zealanders have towards the US for supposedly being our 'Big Brother' when threatened by illusory foreign threats, is based on false assumptions. When William Clark told Australia's Malcolm Fraser several decades ago that this area would not be assisted by the US unless aggression involved a Russian-backed incursion, it was a signal that China was an ally in the containment of the USSR and nothing would be done to interfere with China. Presently there is still no reason to believe that the US has changed that outlook, and post-Soviet Russia remains as much a problem for the US as ever. There seems little evidence also that the US has sought to counter China's penetration into the Pacific by means of 'aid' to the small Pacific states, which are being bought-off with Chinese money and technical assistance. Thereby a string of strategic small island nations has been brought into the Chinese orbit, which will be considered below.

NEW ZEALAND'S PATH TO CHINA STEMS FROM COLD WAR ERA

New Zealand business, officialdom and Government view New Zealand's relationship with China in terms of export markets and as the panacea for New Zealand's economic problems. China sees New Zealand in geopolitical terms, which also happens to coincide with US policy since the days of the Cold War. Russia remains the issue for US and Chinese hegemony, and New Zealand has naively placed itself in the middle of superpower global politics of which it understands nothing.

New Zealand's official relationship with China began under the Labour Government of Norman Kirk when diplomatic relations were established in 1972,[35] the same year as the Kissinger-Nixon 'ping-pong diplomacy.' Although Kirk aimed to establish an independent direction for New Zealand's foreign policy, New Zealand's official relationship began in the same year as the American initiative. The US initiative marked the beginning of China's entry into the 'new world order' as it is now termed.

In 1976, the New Zealand relationship with China as part of a broader US Cold War agenda to 'contain the USSR' was formalised with the visit to Peking of the National Government's Prime Minister Robert Muldoon. Muldoon was avidly anti-Soviet, made a name for himself as a populist opponent of 'communist influence in the trade unions,' an anti-communist who was nonetheless keen to cultivate relationships with America's new Cold War ally, China. It was under Muldoon's regime that Soviet Ambassador Vsevolod Sofinsky was expelled from New Zealand in 1980 for allegedly passing $10,000 to George Jackson, National Secretary of the Moscow-aligned Socialist Unity Party in 1979. Diplomatic relations were not fully re-established until 1984.[36]

When Muldoon travelled to Peking in 1976 to meet Mao Zedong the agenda was plainly stated. China was eager for New Zealand to maintain its alliance with the US and Muldoon as an anti-Soviet Cold Warrior was eager to oblige. Muldoon reported that:

> Mr Hua supported New Zealand and Australian moves to strengthen their defences and hoped that the US would join the two countries on the basis of equality to

---

35 'China and New Zealand, I. Bilateral Political Relationship and major exchange of visits, A. Chinese Visits to New Zealand,' Ministry of Foreign Affairs of the People's Republic of China, http://www.mfa.gov.cn/eng/wjb/zzjg/bmdyzs/gjlb/3412/t17070.htm.

36 Graeme Hunt, *Spies and Revolutionaries: A History of New Zealand Subversion* (Auckland: Reed Publishing, 2007), 252–54.

deal with the 'polar bear' [the USSR]. In other words, he supports the ANZUS concept we have explained to him.[37]

In the year 2000, New Zealand Governor General Michael Hardie Boys went to China to 'set a seal on high-level contact' and reciprocate the visit by Chinese President Jiang Zemin to New Zealand in September 1999. 'He added that the visit will cement bilateral relations at the highest level between the two governments.'[38] New Zealand's ambassador to China, Peter Adams, stated at the time:

> The two countries have regular consultations on security, disarmament and trade and economy, and will extend a similar mechanism to the agricultural sector. The two countries have also increased cooperation in regional and global forums, including the Asia-Pacific Economic Cooperation (APEC) meetings, the Association of Southeast Asian Nations (ASEAN) regional forums and the United Nations.

> 'New Zealand is a practitioner of the one-China policy, and it shares many common perspectives on regional security issues and on the need for economic integration through APEC and the World Trade Organization (WTO),' he said.

> New Zealand was the first Western country to commence bilateral negotiations with China on China's WTO entry, and also the first Western country to conclude such talks in 1997. Therefore, New Zealand is keen to see China join the WTO as soon as possible, he said.[39]

---

37 *The Evening Post* (Wellington, New Zealand), 1 May 1976, 2.

38 'New Zealand Pursue Cooperation with China,' *The Evening Post* (Wellington, New Zealand), ca. October 2000.

39 Ibid.

New Zealanders only really became aware of New Zealand's rapidly developing relationship with China in the several years of negotiations preceding the New Zealand-China Free Trade Agreement of 2008. Yet official bilateral, high level contacts between the two, including military contact, has been what the Chinese Ministry of Foreign Affairs describes as 'frequent' since 1972. The Ministry lists these contacts up until 2003.[40]

In July 2008, New Zealand and Chinese army chiefs met in Beijing. China reported on this high level meeting, which does not seem to have been mentioned by New Zealand media:

> China and New Zealand vowed here on Friday to further army exchanges to push forward military relations between the two countries. 'The Chinese armed forces advocate expanding contact and substantial cooperation with their New Zealand counterparts to upgrade military relations in the long run,' said Chen Bingde, Chief of the General Staff of the Chinese People's Liberation Army.[41]

Few know of the extensive military and foreign policy contacts. Hence when Professor David Shambaugh of George Washington University, an authority on China and international security and politics of the Asia-Pacific region, visited New Zealand to address the annual Otago University Foreign Policy School in June, 'he was astonished by New Zealand's naiveté about its relationship with China.'[42] He commented that while academic interest in China is

---

40 'China and New Zealand,' Ministry of Foreign Affairs of the People's Republic of China, 26 August 2003, http://www.mfa.gov.cn/eng/wjb/zzjg/bmdyzs/gjlb/3412/t17070.htm.

41 'China, New Zealand Pledge to Further Army Exchanges,' www.chinaview.cn, 4 July 2008.

42 John Hartevelt, 'Eyes Wide Shut on Our Asian Integration,' *The Dominion Post* (Wellington, New Zealand), 3 July 2010, A9.

strong in New Zealand, 'it has no real strategic direction.' Shambaugh believes that certain strategic assets should be off-limits to foreign ownership. New Zealand ought to consider the possibility of China demanding access to extract minerals. New Zealand has not, he says, properly considered that China might ask to formally call on Kiwi ports with its naval ships.

However this already occurs. The destroyer *Haerbin*, accompanied by its supply ship *Hongzehu*, called at Wellington and other ports in October 2007, after having been involved in exercises with Australian and New Zealand ships. At the same time the New Zealand frigate *Te Kaha* was berthed at the People's Liberation Army Navy wharf in Shanghai. *Te Kaha* was to undertake an exercise with a similar sized Chinese ship. *Te Kaha*'s commander Andy Grant stated, 'Such exercises were important to the military relationship.' He stated, 'The level of engagement is quite high both ways.'[43] Commander Grant continued:

> New Zealanders in general are not aware of what their military forces are doing. It's not a big part of the New Zealand psyche. We get a lot of delegations from the Chinese armed forces coming to New Zealand, but I don't think that's generally well known.[44]

New Zealand Maritime Component Commander, Commodore David Anson, stationed in Shanghai, stated: 'There's no doubt that New Zealand is wishing to grow its relationship with China—there's no doubt in all facets. Military is just one of those building blocs.'[45]

Professor Shambaugh's visit prompted one of the few

---

43   'Flying the Flag in China,' *The Dominion Post* (Wellington, New Zealand), 15
      October 2007, 1.

44   Ibid.

45   Ibid.

features on China in a major newspaper dealing with matters other than the strictly economic. Yet here too the focus was primarily on how inexorable our relationship is with China and any opposition is called, in Prime Minister John Key's words, 'xenophobia.' Hence, even here, the insights that Shambaugh might have been able to give received scant notice. What *The Dominion Post* article did provide, however, were four numbered points summarising prime facets of the Sino-New Zealand relationship. Among the four were:

3. Diplomacy. New Zealand enjoys a strong relationship with the United States and China considers its relationship with the US a high priority. China thinks that New Zealand can play a positive role in bridging its gap with the US.

4. Geopolitical. China wants to secure good relations with as many countries in the South Pacific as possible. It wants to secure Taiwan, and Taiwan enjoys good friendships with many of the small island countries. New Zealand has influence over those nations, so closer ties could improve China's relations with them.[46]

These couple of points are about as near to reality as New Zealanders are likely to read anywhere in the mainstream media. The US decided decades ago to allow the Pacific region to become one of China's spheres of influence. Since the geopolitical situation of the Cold War era has not fundamentally altered because of the intransigence of post-Soviet Russia in not subordinating herself to globalisation, there is no reason to believe that US policy towards this region vis-à-vis China has changed, and it makes sense from a geopolitical perspective to have China continue expanding in the region to 'contain Russia' as in the Soviet days of the Cold War. Moreover, if the US thought there was danger

---

46 Hartevelt, 'Eyes Wide Shut on Our Asian Integration.'

to its geopolitical strategies in New Zealand's relationship with China, it seems likely that the US would be applying pressure to New Zealand to change its direction. Hence, the US seems satisfied for New Zealand's relationship with China to continue developing as part of the globalist process for regionalisation.

New Zealand thereby serves as China's proxy in the South Pacific, and would more likely be looked on as a big brother than a fire-breathing, all-consuming dragon. The importance of this region has been indicated by a White Paper issued by China on 17 October 2000 that demarcates 'first and second lines of island defence' in the Pacific. The first line of defence runs from Taiwan through the Spratly Islands to Singapore. The first island-chains describe the sphere of influence that China expects to achieve in the Pacific Ocean. According to the White Paper China plans to upgrade its navy to permit it to control 'what its military calls "the first island-chain" by 2010 and to "the second island-chain" by 2040.' 'The first island-chain includes Japan, Okinawa, Taiwan, the Philippines and Brunei. The second island-chain extends to Australia's doorsteps.' Shen Dingli, an expert on the Chinese military at Fudan University, Shanghai, stated: 'Once the Taiwan front is closed, we may turn to the South China Sea,' [Beyond the South China Sea], 'we have a third issue to resolve, namely to take the Diaoyutai Islands from Japan.'[47] As we have considered previously, Diaoyutai, the Chinese name for the Senkaku Islands, was the subject of Chinese naval incursions in 2012.

China is continually expanding its presence in the Pacific region by bribes of aid and trade with the small island nations to fulfil these plans. Chinese influence has been bought in Tonga, Fiji, Nauru, Papua New Guinea, and

---

47   Phil Brennan, 'China Rebuilds Its Military Muscle,' *NewsMax*, 19 October 2002, http://archive.newsmax.com/archives/articles/2002/10/18/165743.shtml.

Vanuatu in the Polynesian and Melanesian areas. In New Zealand, of particular note among the Chinese investments, Li Ka Shing's Cheung Kong Infrastructure bought Vector, the Wellington power grid, in 2008. Vector was sold to Li Ka on the advice of Goldman Sachs,[48] which itself is one of those global movers-and-shakers which has had a close relationship with China since the 1970s, and in 2004 became the first international bank to be permitted to arrange equity and bond deals in China. Goldman Sachs is also associated with Mr Li's Hutchison Whampoa Ltd. The importance of Li is not that he is China's richest businessman, but what seems to be a close association with Chinese military, his corporations specialising in buying up strategic assets throughout the world. Hutchison Whampoa Limited operationally controls the Panama Canal, and has built the largest container port in the world at Freeport, Bahamas. Li is a board member of the China International Trust and Investment Corporation, used as a front by China's military to acquire technology for weapons development. When Li buys an asset he is therefore doing so with a lot more in mind than merely profit.

US HEGEMONY

The US is not a natural leader of any Western bloc, 'the Western world' or alliance with Europe. It is and always has been a misnomer to call the US the 'leader of the Western world.' The US has since the time of President Woodrow Wilson regarded Europe as its vassal. The US sought to unite Europe on American terms. America's global agenda largely proceeds from cultural subversion, which is antithetical to traditional Western culture, and indeed to all traditional cultures. Significantly, India is one of the few states in the world which has managed to maintain her traditional culture despite the demands that will be increasingly made on her by globalisation and 'free trade.' Tradition-based states are

48   *The Dominion Post* (Wellington, New Zealand), 29 April 2008, C1.

161

obstacles to globalisation and are marked for destruction by 'colour revolutions' that receive funding and training from such organisations as Soros' Open Society network, the National Endowment for Democracy, Freedom House, and a vast array of other think tanks and NGOs that include luminaries from the US foreign policy and business sectors. If they do not succumb to subversion and continue to resist globalisation, they can eventually be bombed into submission, as with the case of Serbia.

Russia struggles to revive her culture, and almost collapsed during the Gorbachev-Yeltsin interregnum. The Putin regime attempts to restore the place of Russian tradition, in which the Orthodox Church is pivotal, just as Hinduism is pivotal to India.

The support given to the likes of 'Pussy Riot' in its denigration not only of Putin but more importantly of the Russian Orthodox Church, is symptomatic of the place cultural decay has in promoting a monocultural world around a money axis. A Catholic traditionalist, conservative columnist, the late Joseph Sobran, cogently expressed the conservative outlook in opposing US global hegemony, which is the real conservative position in contrast to the misnamed 'neo-conservatives.' He pointed out that opposition to what the Left has called 'American cultural imperialism' is something that must be opposed with vigour by conservatives and traditionalists of all nations:

> The United States is now a global empire that wants to think of itself as a universal benefactor, and is nonplussed when foreigners don't see it that way. None of the earlier empires of this world, as far as I know, shared this delusion; the Romans, the Mongols, the British, the Russians and Soviets didn't expect to rule and to be loved at the same time. Why do we?[49]

---

49   Joseph Sobran, 'How Many Enemies Do We Want?,' November 1999. Retrieved

The answer is that the US is a messianic state. It has its own world mission to spread what is called the 'American Dream.' Its uniquely American interpretation of Christianity is called the 'profit gospel,' a religion that can be traced to the Puritan foundations of the US, and Puritanism was the preferred religion of merchants. The 'profit gospel' states that wealth is a blessing from God; which is the same as the Puritan ethic. Hence American geopolitics and wars are described in religious terms, that is, in terms of 'saving the world.' The secular religion that the US seeks to impose over the world is the type of 18th-century liberalism that sees individuals as primarily concerned with commerce, whose 'rights' are contractual, legalistic and not based on tradition or ethos.

US global hegemony is undertaken by cultural subversion as a means of opening a state up to globalism through the use of what can be seen as a 'global culture.' Major Ralph Peters outlined the cultural offensive in an article for *Parameters* in 1997. Here Peters states that the world is 'entering a new American century,' in which America's increased power will be concomitant with being 'culturally more lethal.' He alludes to the 'clash of civilisations' and democracy as the 'liberal form of imperialism.' Peters wrote of how America would dominate through cultural subversion, stating:

Hollywood goes where Harvard never penetrated. . . . American culture is the most powerful in history, and the most destructive competitor of cultures. . . . Our military power is culturally based. . . . For the majority of our citizens, our vulgar, near-chaotic, marvellous culture is the greatest engine of positive change in history . . . But American culture is infectious, a plague of pleasure . . . But Hollywood is 'preparing the battlefield,' and burgers precede bullets. The flag follows trade . . .[50]

---

from http://www.iraqwar.org/sobran.htm.

50   Ralph Peters, 'Constant Conflict,' *Parameters: US Army College Quarterly*, vol. 27,

Peters, who retired in 1998 as a Lieutenant Colonel, entitled the article 'Constant Conflict,' when he was attached to the Office of the Deputy Chief of Staff for Intelligence. He continues to be a commentator and writer on military strategy and foreign policy. Hence the traditional critique from the Left of 'American cultural imperialism' is now just as much a concern for the traditional (palaeo-) conservative, and for those who uphold traditional cultures everywhere.

RUSSIA AND THE US

Russia is the major obstacle to this globalist hegemony, as it was under Stalin onward.[51] One of the numerous globalist NGOs directed against Russia, the Jamestown Foundation,[52] offered several opinions in regard to the direction of Russia with Putin's re-election in 2011. A major concern is whether Putin's anti-American expressions during the elections were based on electoral rhetoric in drumming up Russians against an external enemy, or a genuinely held perception of the US as intrinsically inimical to Russia. Certainly Putin would be naïve if he regards the US as anything other than being committed to the subordination of Russia to economic predation and cultural decay. The US has been the home-base for the destruction of Russia as a world power since Stalin's rejection of the US's vision of the post-war world in 1945, inaugurating the 'Cold War.'[53] The very fact of the existence of the Jamestown Foundation, among a gaggle of other NGOs whose board members often have close connections with US governmental agencies, including the military and intelligence,[54] indicates this.

---

no. 2, Summer 1997, 4–14.

51   Cf. K. R. Bolton, *Stalin: The Enduring Legacy*, inter alia.

52   The Jamestown Foundation, 'Mission,' http://www.jamestown.org/aboutus/.

53   K. R. Bolton, 'Origins of the Cold War: How Stalin Foiled a New World Order,' 31 May 2010, http://www.foreignpolicyjournal.com/2010/05/31/origins-of-the-cold-war-how-stalin-foild-a-new-world-order/. K. R. Bolton, *Stalin: The Enduring Legacy* (London: Black House Publishing, 2012), 125–39.

54   See, for example, the Jamestown Foundation's board members: 'Board Members,'

Citing a report from Chatham House by James Nixey, entitled 'Russia's Geopolitical Compass,' Nixey points to four 'geostrategic axes for Russia: the West, Russia's many 'souths'—the Black Sea region and the Islamic world—Russia's Far East and the Arctic North.' Nixey states that Russia no longer views the 'West' as all-powerful, and that Obama's post-Bush so-called 'Reset' policy for rapprochement with Russia is 'losing direction.' What is particularly interesting is that Nixey agrees with Bobo Lo 'that Russia's relations with China are nothing more than an "alliance of convenience" by which Russia seeks to leverage influence with the West to gain acceptance. In this context, China is only a "geopolitical counterweight to the West."'[55]

There are those both on the 'fringes' of politics and in influential positions who see Russia as an ally rather than as a threat to a united Europe. France having more than the usual number of geopolitical realists has included a strong Russophile element that looked to Russia, including during its Soviet days, as a counterweight to US hegemony contrary to the propaganda of the Soviet bogeyman poised to ravish the Occident. One probably most immediately recalls the advocacy by President Charles de Gaulle for a united Europe 'from the Atlantic to the Urals.' The Jamestown Foundation's article cites a view offered by Marc Rousset, a French historian and political analyst, in contrast to those whose vision of a 'Eurasian' bloc still focuses on China as an ally:

According to Rousset, Putin would bring 'bravery, foresight and pragmatism' to Russian policy in the interest of creating a geopolitical order from the Atlantic to Vladivostok. Rousset emphasized that Putin is a

http://www.jamestown.org/aboutus/boardmembers/.

55   Jacob W. Kipp, 'The Elections Are Over and Putin Won: Whither Russia?,' 30 March 2012, http://www.jamestown.org/programs/edm/single/?tx_ttnews[tt_news]=39215&cHash=5bc45dc36c8f713aa6f5e393e5eae5b4.

European from St. Petersburg working toward closer ties among Russia, Ukraine and Belarus. His conception of a Eurasian union had the possibility of creating an imperial order to rival that of the American empire and the emerging new orders in China and India[56] (*Rossiiskaia Gazeta*, March 6). Rousset was quoted in November of last year as seeing the emergence of an axis of Paris, Berlin and Moscow being the answer to the present crisis in the Eurozone and the means to restore Europe's position as a major player in the international system (*Rossiiskaia Gazeta*, November 17, 2011). Sergei Karganov answered that line of thought in December of last year by calling on Russia to turn away from Europe and make its future with a dynamic Asia-Pacific region led by China (*Rossiiskaia Gazeta*, December 28, 2011).[57]

US actions against Putin's Russia remain as determined as those against the USSR during the Cold War. Dr. Paul Craig Roberts, US Assistant Secretary of the Treasury under the Reagan Administration, has written of US-sponsored subversion against Russia:

> The Russian government has finally caught on that its political opposition is being financed by the US taxpayer-funded National Endowment for Democracy and other CIA/State Department fronts in an attempt to subvert the Russian government and install an American puppet state in the geographically largest country on earth, the one country with a nuclear arsenal sufficient to deter Washington's aggression.[58]

Roberts was referring to an Act passed by the Duma

---

56 There is no geopolitical imperative for rivalry between Russia and India, but rather the continuation of the historical alignment between them.

57 Kipp, op. cit., citing Marc Rousset, *La nouvelle Europe: Paris-Berlin-Moscou* (Paris: Godefroy de Bouillon, 2009).

58 Paul Craig Roberts, 'War on All Fronts,' *Foreign Policy Journal*, 19 July 2012, http://www.foreignpolicyjournal.com/2012/07/19/war-on-all-fronts/.

requiring the registration of NGOs receiving foreign funds, similar to the requirements of US laws that have long been in place.[59] Roberts continues:

> The Washington-funded Russian political opposition masquerades behind 'human rights' and says it works to 'open Russia.' What the disloyal and treasonous Washington-funded Russian 'political opposition' means by 'open Russia' is to open Russia for brainwashing by Western propaganda, to open Russia to economic plunder by the West, and to open Russia to having its domestic and foreign policies determined by Washington.[60]

Globalists are aiming to deconstruct Russia as they did the USSR. Fortunately, Putin is no Gorbachev. His ambition seems to be that of leading a strong Russia, as distinct from Mikhail Gorbachev's ambition to become a globalist celebrity posturing on the world stage. When Hollywood stars hosted a 'gala celebration' at the Royal Albert Hall in London on his 80th birthday in 2011, ABC News commented that the 'movie stars, singers and politicians' who turned out for the show 'underlined the celebrity status Mr Gorbachev enjoys in the West, where he is widely perceived as the man who freed Eastern Europe from Soviet rule and ended the Cold War.'[61] On the occasion of his birthday Gorbachev delivered what might be construed as an ultimatum to Putin on behalf of the globalist elite, 'advising' him 'against running for a third term as president and warning about the dangers of Arab-style social revolt.'[62] As is now clear, those 'Arab social

---

59 'Duma Committee Supports Ban on NGO Using US Grants,' *Russia and India Report*, 18 December 2012, http://indrus.in/articles/2012/12/18/duma_committee_supports_ban_on_ngo_using_us_grants_21103.html.

60 Ibid.

61 Reuters, *ABC News*, 'Stars Honour Gorbachev at Gala Birthday Bash,' 31 March 2011, http://www.abc.net.au/news/stories/2011/03/31/3178823.htm.

62 Hagit Klaiman, 'Peres Attends Gorbachev's Birthday Bash in London,' 31 March 2011, http://www.ynetnews.com/articles/0,7340,L-4050192,00.html.

revolts,' like the 'colour revolutions' in the former Soviet states, were stage-managed by the globalist NGOs.

The globalist think tanks are blatant in their intentions. The Council on Foreign Relations (CFR) opines that 'Russia is heading in the wrong direction.'[63] One of the CFR's recommendations is to interfere with the Russian political process, urging US Congress to fund opposition movements by increased funding for the *Freedom Support Act*, in this instance referring specifically to the 2007–2008 presidential elections.[64] Authors of the CFR report include Mark F. Brzezinski, who served on the National Security Council as an adviser on Russian and Eurasian affairs under Clinton, as his father Zbigniew served in the Carter Administration; Antonia W. Bouis, founding executive director of the Soros Foundations; James A. Harmon, senior advisor to the Rothschild Group, et al.

The task of publicly announcing the post-Soviet world revolution was allotted to President George W. Bush. Speaking before the National Endowment for Democracy in 2003, Bush stated that the war on Iraq was a continuation of a 'world democratic revolution' that started in the Soviet bloc: 'The revolution under former president Ronald Reagan freed the people of Soviet-dominated Europe, he declared, and is destined now to liberate the Middle East as well.'[65]

Gorbachev had prepared the deconstruction of the Soviet bloc in 1988, when he announced to the United Nations

---

63   Jack Kemp et al., *Russia's Wrong Direction: What the United States Can and Should Do*, Independent Task Force Report, no. 57 (New York: Council on Foreign Relations, 2006), xi. The publication can be downloaded at: http://www.cfr.org/publication/9997/.

64   Ibid.

65   Fred Barbash, 'Bush: Iraq Part of "Global Democratic Revolution": Liberation of Middle East Portrayed as Continuation of Reagan's Policies,' *Washington Post*, 6 November 2003.

General Assembly a reversal of Soviet policy: Russia would not come to the defence of Warsaw Pact regimes in the event of revolt. Immediately after he met President Reagan and President-elect George Bush.[66]

The subverting of post-Soviet Russia has proceeded no less vigorously. Carl Gershman, president of the National Endowment for Democracy (NED), remarked that the Solidarity movement in Poland was created the year following Gorbachev's United Nations speech, and set in motion the dismantling of the Soviet bloc, which he termed 'a new concept of incremental democratic enlargement,' which the NED calls 'cross-border work.'[67] This had its origins 'in a conference that was sponsored by the Polish-Czech-Slovak Solidarity Foundation in Wroclaw in early November of 1989.'[68] This movement continues to the present, Gershman stating:

> And so cross-border work was born, and it has continued to expand ever since. The Polish-Czech-Slovak Solidarity Foundation went from providing support for desktop publishing in the Czech Republic and Slovakia to providing similar aid in Ukraine and Belarus, and today it works in Russia, Moldova, the Caucasus and Central Asia. Other Polish groups also engage in cross-border work, from the Foundation for Education for Democracy, an outgrowth of the Solidarity Teachers Union which provides training in civic education for teachers and NGO leaders throughout the former Soviet Union, to the East European Democratic Center which

---

66 Dr. Svetlana Savranskaya and Thomas Blanton, eds., 'Previously Secret Documents from Soviet and U.S. Files on the 1988 Summit in New York, 20 Years Later,' National Security Archive Electronic Briefing Book No. 261, 8 December 2008.

67 Carl Gershman, 'Giving Solidarity to the World,' Georgetown University, 19 May 2009, http://www.ned.org/about/board/meet-our-president/archived-remarks-and-presentations/051909.

68 Ibid.

supports local media in Ukraine and Central Asia.[69]

Just prior to Gorbachev's warning to Putin against standing for re-election, Gershman had commented that:

> . . . Putin may be in control in Russia, but he has lost the support of the political elite which fears that his return to the presidency will usher in a period of Brezhnev-like stagnation and continued economic and societal decline . . . International groups should be prepared to provide whatever assistance is needed and desired by local actors. Areas of support would include party development and election administration and monitoring, strengthening civil society and independent media, and making available the expertise of specialists in such fields as constitutionalism and electoral law as well as the experience of participants in earlier transitions.[70]

It was an unequivocal call to overthrow Putin. The rivalry between the US and Russia today is as marked as it was during the Cold War. Putin scuttled Washington and Wall Street plans for Russia in the aftermath of the Soviet collapse in a way reminiscent of Stalin's scuttling of US plans for Russia in the aftermath of World War II.

RUSSIA AND THE NEW WORLD ORDER

Putin has embraced 'Eurasianism' as the alternative to a 'new world order' based around US hegemony. In a major foreign policy article in 2012, Putin outlined the major premises: He stated that Russian would be guided by her own interests first, based on Russia's strength, and would not be dictated to by outsiders. He questions the US missiles being placed

---

69   Ibid.

70   Carl Gershman, 'The Fourth Wave: Where the Middle East Revolts Fit in the History of Democratization—and How We Can Support Them,' 14 March 2011, http://www.tnr.com/article/world/85143/middle-east-revolt-democratization.

on Russia's borders, and the continuing belligerence of NATO, stating that 'The Americans have become obsessed with the idea of becoming absolutely invulnerable.'[71] Importantly, Putin is fully aware that globalist agendas are being imposed behind the façade of 'human rights,' and criticises the selectivity with which this morality is applied: 'The recent series of armed conflicts started under the pretext of humanitarian aims is undermining the time-honoured principle of state sovereignty, creating a moral and legal void in the practice of international relations.'[72] Putin refers to the 'Arab Spring,' noting outside interference in a 'domestic conflict.' 'The revolting slaughter of Muammar Gaddafi . . . was primeval,' Putin states, and the Libyan scenario should not be repeated in Syria. He adds of the 'regime changes':

It appears that with the Arab Spring countries, as with Iraq, Russian companies are losing their decades-long positions in local commercial markets and are being deprived of large commercial contracts. The niches thus vacated are being filled by the economic operatives of the states that had a hand in the change of the ruling regime. One could reasonably conclude that tragic events have been encouraged to a certain extent by someone's interest in a re-division of the commercial market rather than a concern for human rights.[73]

Putin sees Russia developing her historic relations with the Arab states, despite the 'regime changes.' He also points out the political uses that are being made of social media which played such a significant role in mobilising and agitating masses during the 'Arab Spring,' and indeed in the 'colour

---

71   Vladimir Putin, 'Russia and the Changing World,' RIA Novosti, 27 February 2012, http://en.rian.ru/world/20120227/171547818.html.

72   Ibid.

73   Ibid.

revolutions' on Russia's doorstep.[74] Putin also acknowledges the subversive role of the NGOs, not least of whose actions are being directed against Russia, stating: '. . . the activities of "pseudo-NGOs" and other agencies that try to destabilize other countries with outside support are unacceptable.' He remarks on the failure of US and NATO intervention in Afghanistan and mentions Russia's historic relationship there,[75] which, it can be added, was eliminated by US backing for the same 'Islamists' that the US now claims to be fighting in a global 'war on terrorism,' indicating the duplicitous, or dialectical, nature of US foreign policy.

While Russia is seen as having an important role in the Asia-Pacific region, and Putin stresses alignment with a strong China, at least for public consumption on the world stage, he also declares:

> Russia is an inalienable and organic part of Greater Europe and European civilization. Our citizens think of themselves as Europeans. We are by no means indifferent to developments in united Europe. That is why Russia proposes moving toward the creation of a common economic and human space from the Atlantic to the Pacific Ocean—a community referred by Russian experts to as 'the Union of Europe,' which will strengthen Russia's potential and position in its economic pivot toward the 'new Asia.'[76]

Putin refers to an exciting new vision of a bloc expanding from 'Lisbon to Vladivostok.' He sees Russia's acceptance to membership of the World Trade Organization as 'symbolic,' while defending Russia's interests. With Russia looking at

---

74 See also: K. R. Bolton, 'Twitterers of the World Revolution: The Digital New-New Left,' *Foreign Policy Journal*, 28 February 2011, http://www.foreignpolicyjournal.com/2011/02/28/twitterers-of-the-world-revolution-the-digital-new-new-left/. Also: K. R. Bolton, *Revolution from Above*, 235–40.

75 Putin, 'Russia and the Changing World.'

76 Ibid.

the Indo-Pacific region, will she be a nexus between this region and Europe, or will she enter the region as a junior partner with China? Some geopolitical analysts are referring to a new geopolitical bloc, challenging both the US and China, as Eurosiberia[77] rather than as Eurasia.

The US is directing itself toward Asia and the Pacific, as per Rockefeller-Trilateralist aims. So far, while Putin alludes to territorial disputes having been settled with China,[78] the Chinese have had everything their own way without significant concessions.

US Secretary of Defense Leon Panetta states that the 'global centre of gravity' is shifting to this region.[79] The US is trying to displace Russia's historic relationship with India by entering into defence contracts, etc.[80] However, India's relationship with Russia is strong and Indian statesmanship realistic. Panetta stresses that US interests in the region do not conflict with those of China. He points to China as having been invited to multilateral military exercises in 2013 and as having 'been invited to send ships to Rimpac[81] in 2014.' Panetta emphasises that the rebalance of US policy is not directed at China, but seeks 'a continuous military-to-military relationship, and stronger defence ties with China and other countries throughout the region.'[82] While Panetta favourably mentions China and other states in the Pacific, no mention is made of Russia, despite her having hosted the APEC Summit in 2012.

77 Guillaume Faye, 'The Geopolitics of Ethnopolitics: The New Concept of "Eurosiberia,"' Counter-Currents Publishing, http://www.counter-currents.com/2010/08/faye-on-eurosiberia/.

78 Putin, op. cit.

79 Leon Panetta, 'United States Strategy Will Refocus on Asia and Pacific,' The Dominion Post (Wellington, New Zealand), 2 January 2013.

80 Ibid.

81 Rimpac = the Rim of Pacific Exercise, 'the world's largest international maritime exercise.' http://www.cpf.navy.mil/rimpac/2012/

82 L. Panetta, op. cit.

RUSSIA AS THE FOCUS FOR AN
ANTI-GLOBALIST BLOC

In the pursuit of American globalism and cultural penetration, Russia represents the primary axis for a European bloc if it is based around states that are historically resistant to US hegemony over Europe, such as France, a major player in the European Union. Any repudiation of a unipolar world based on US hegemony again centres on Russia, whose regime after the US-orientated Yeltsin era aims to restore Russian influence. The alliance between China and Russia is contrary to history and ethnography and will not last. It is not a natural geopolitical alliance, for reasons already explained.

One very real scenario for regional crisis is that of a Chinese confrontation with India, Russia and Central Asia in a struggle for resources, especially that of water. Central Asia, India and other states as far away as Vietnam will gravitate towards Russia as China becomes increasingly hegemonic.

A Latin American bloc is emerging around Venezuela. Combined, a Latin American bloc would have immense resources. A 'Bolivarian' revolution was initiated throughout Latin America under the inspiration of the late Hugo Chavez of Venezuela. Those opposed to a unipolar world can only hope that the Bolivarian revolution will maintain its impetus despite Chavez's recent death. This Latin American bloc has been forming in defiance of North American hegemonic ambitions, and was launched as 'The Bolivarian Alternative for the People of Our America' (ALBA) in 2004 by Venezuela and Cuba as an alternative to the US-backed 'Free Trade Area of the Americas.' By June 2009, ALBA had grown to nine member states, and the name was changed to the 'Bolivarian Alliance for the People of Our America.' A Latin American bloc will seek alignment with Russia to counter US pressure, and Venezuela is already doing so.

Russian geopolitical theorist Alexander Dugin is currently the most active exponent of the concept of 'Eurasianism.' Eurasianism is not a new concept. It has had exponents not only in Russia but also particularly in Germany during the Weimar period. Even during the era of the Bolshevik regime in Russia, a certain faction of German conservatives considered an alliance with Russia to be a natural development in the face of the imposition of the Versailles Treaty by the Western powers. The Treaty of Rapallo (1922) signed between Russia and Germany, which extended to covert military cooperation, was one such manifestation of this tendency among influential German circles to circumvent the strictures of the Versailles Treaty.

During the Weimar period geopolitical theorist Karl Haushofer advocated an alliance between Germany and Russia. Haushofer might be regarded as a precursor of Dugin insofar as he advocated the 'great spaces' and geopolitical blocs of the type now being advocated by Dugin. The Haushofer school of *geopolitik* came to advocate Eurasianism centred on a Russo-German alliance that could counter Anglo-American world power, which was considered to be the axis for plutocracy.[83] Dugin today talks in similar terms, and sees Eurasianism as a counter-balance to the 'Atlanticism' of the Anglo-American powers[84] although 'plutocratic powers' might be a better term as the doctrine they spread is not rooted in any particular culture other than profit, and while the City of London remains one of the major centres of plutocracy, nothing is left of Britain *per se* as a world power.

Even now among high-level European sources, there is a tendency towards such an alliance with Russia, cogently

83 Johannes Mattern, *Geopolitik: Doctrine of National Self-Sufficiency and Empire* (Baltimore, MD: Johns Hopkins University Press, 1942), 40–41.

84 A. Dugin, 'The Eurasian Idea,' *Ab Aeterno*, Academy of Social and Political Research, no. 1, November 2009.

expressed by Olivier Védrine, founder of the think tank 'Atlantique Oural College.' Védrine considers Russia to be European. He alludes to the ageing Russian population in comparison to the burgeoning Chinese population in Eastern Siberia. Védrine opposes the criticism of the Western media in regard to Russia's not having fully embraced 'liberal democracy,' and states that political models cannot and should not be transplanted as a universal model. Védrine writes of a pan-European unity embracing Russia:

> This lack of comprehension leads to misunderstandings which can only be negative for Europe as a whole and could lead to a new political barrier running across the heart of Europe. In these times of global geopolitical uncertainty we do not need new divisions in Europe but a tightening of the ranks behind a united front![85]

In a dichotomy that sets Mongol Asia against Slavic Russia and alludes to a commonality of outlook between Russia and Europe in regard to what is today the rise of China, Védrine draws on the rise of Mongol-Tatar rule over Russia from the thirteenth century, and states that Russia regards its sacrifices under that rule as having saved Europe 'from the Tatar-Mongol yoke of servitude.'[86] Védrine reviews the epochal events of Russian history from Mongol domination to the present Putin era, which he sees as having revived Russia out of the 'economic collapse marked by the Yeltsin years.' Védrine states that before the 'colour revolutions' of the 1990s, which generated renewed Russian distrust, Russia had considered an arrangement with the European Union to counter US influence in Europe, especially militarily.

The confrontation with Georgia over South Ossetia, with

85 Olivier Védrine, 'Russia Is Indeed a European Country,' September 2009, retrieved from http://collegeatlantiqueoural.

86 Ibid.

the US and some European countries backing Georgia, has deepened Russian mistrust. Védrine calls for a building of alliances of common geopolitical interest between Europe and Russia, and states that any division will cause 'pleasure and advantage' to Europe's rivals. He ends by calling for an alliance in the traditional terminology of Eurasianism: a 'Paris-Berlin-Moscow axis': 'A Europe reflecting the vision of General Charles de Gaulle: From the Atlantic to the Urals passing through the axis of Paris-Berlin-Moscow!' Védrine is cited here because he provides an example of how the concept of a Eurasian alliance is far from obsolete historically, or merely the preserve of fringe political elements, but continues to have influential proponents.

In Russia, Alexander Dugin is the principal proponent of Eurasianism, and his influence reaches further afield, to the extent of his having inspired the founding of an International Eurasian Movement that has adherents beyond Russia. Two antagonistic academics commented on Dugin's influence: 'The growing interest among political scientists and other observers in Dugin and his activities is the result of his recent evolution from a little-known marginal radical right-winger to a notable and seemingly influential figure within Russia's mainstream.'[87]

The International Eurasian Movement was founded in Moscow in 2003. Something of its influence is indicated from its founding Supreme Council, some of whose members under the chairmanship of Dugin, include: E. D. Kokoity, President of the Republic of South Ossetia; A. P. Torshin, Vice-Speaker of the Russian Federation's Federation Council; A. A. Aslakhanov, Assistant to the President of Russia; T. S. Tajuddin, Supreme Mufti of the Central Spiritual Board of Muslims of Russia and

87 Anton Shekhovtsov and Andreas Umland, 'Is Aleksandr Dugin a Traditionalist? "Neo-Eurasianism" and Perennial Philosophy,' *The Russian Review*, no. 68, October 2009, 662–78.

European CIS countries; A. S. Borisov, Minister of Culture of the Republic of Sakha (Yakutia), Rector of the Arctic National Institute of Culture and Arts; General Pierre-Marie Gallois (France); V. I. Kaljuzhnyj, Ambassador Extraordinary and Plenipotentiary of the Russian Federation; A. J. Dzhumagulov, Ambassador Extraordinary and Plenipotentiary Ambassador of the Republic of Kyrgyzstan; A. S. Chernyshev, Ambassador Extraordinary and Plenipotentiary Ambassador of Russia, Chairman of the Council of ambassadors, President of the Company Russo-Turkish friendship; E. V. Matusevich, Director of the Academy of Management under the President of the Republic of Belarus, the Director of the Research Institute of the theory and practice of government of the Republic of Belarus; V. I. Nifadiev, Rector of the Kyrgyz-Russia Slavic University (Kyrgyzstan, Bishkek); M. K. Esenov, Director, Centre for Socio-Political Studies, 'Central Asia and Caucasus' (Sweden); T. Z. Rysbekov, Rector of West-Kazakhstan State University; D. Perinçek, Chairman, Working Party of Turkey; et al.

Dugin's concept of Eurasianism however extends beyond Europe and Russia as he seeks to formulate it as a globally applicable geopolitical paradigm. As the above membership of the founding Supreme Council of the International Eurasian Movement indicates, Eurasianism has a widespread and influential following. Other members of the council come from Serbia, France, Japan and Italy. Dugin's theory arises from the post-Cold War era that saw the collapse of Russia as a world power under Gorbachev and Yeltsin, and its present re-emergence under Putin; amidst globalisation and what is called by Dugin the 'unipolar world,' where global power centres around one axis, that of the US, with others in subordinate positions (with the exception of an emergent China).

Somewhat akin to Charles de Gaulle's concept of a 'Europe

from the Atlantic to the Urals,' and the similar principle being advocated now by Olivier Védrine, Dugin seeks a power bloc in a Euro-Russian alliance that will challenge US global hegemony, or rather make it redundant. However Dugin goes further, and applies his geopolitical theory to the potential emergence of a number of power blocs or 'meridians.' He sees some type of globalisation as the *zeitgeist* of this era. Whether this globalisation will be in the form of a 'new world order'[88] under US suzerainty, or in the form of large self-contained geopolitical formations, is the question that has yet to be decided. Dugin writes of the international application of his version of Eurasianism:

> In the broad sense the Eurasian Idea and even the Eurasian concept do not strictly correspond to the geopolitical boundaries of the Eurasian continent. The Eurasian Idea is a global-scale strategy that acknowledges the objectivity of globalisation and the termination of nation-states, but at the same time offers a different scenario of globalisation, which entails no unipolar world or united global government. Instead it offers several global zones (poles). The Eurasian Idea is an alternative or multipolar version of globalisation, but globalisation is the currently fundamental world process that is deciding the main vector of modern history.[89]

What Dugin calls a 'pluriverse' of geopolitical blocs would comprise, as he envisages it, an integrated Europe and the Russian Federation,[90] a Russian alliance with Turkey and certain Mongolian and Caucasian nations, and the division of the world into 'four meridian zones.' Under this geopolitical orientation there would be: An 'Atlantic meridian zone' of the two American continents within the 'framework of the Monroe Doctrine'; a Euro-Africa zone

---

88   Dugin, 'The Eurasian Idea,' 33.
89   Ibid., 32.
90   Ibid., 35.

with the European Union as its centre; a Russian-Central Asian zone; and a Pacific zone.

Within these geopolitical groupings 'Hindustan' would constitute one of the 'Great spaces' as a self-dependent civilization sector.'[91] The 'Pacific meridian zone' would be dominated by China and Japan, and would include Australia, although Dugin mentions that some researchers would place Australia in the 'American meridian zone.'[92] From this it must be assumed that New Zealand would also be placed in the 'Pacific meridian zone.'

AN ANZAC-RUSSO-INDIAN ALLIANCE?

Dugin's world geopolitical model presents some problems. However, Dugin's paradigm does not rest on intractable dogma, and he states that it is open to adjustments. Dugin writes: 'Eurasianism is an open, non-dogmatic philosophy that can be enriched with new content.'[93]

Dugin's Eurasianism is thus adjusted by new input from religion, sociological and ethnological discoveries, economics, national geography, culture, strategic and political research, and so on.[94] There are four principles of Dugin's Eurasianism: (1) 'differentialism' or 'pluralism' rather than one dominant global system; (2) traditionalism; rights of nations versus global economic interests; (3) ethnicities versus the depersonalisation of nations into 'artificial social constructs'; and (4) social justice as opposed to exploitation.[95]

Into the broad geopolitical blocs proposed by Dugin there are numerous sub-alliances. As far as this impacts on

91 Ibid., 36.
92 Ibid.
93 Ibid., 40.
94 Ibid.
95 Ibid.

Australia and New Zealand what is of specific interest is that under Dugin's system Australia (and by implication New Zealand) would become part of either a Pacific meridian zone necessarily dominated by China, or possibly part of the Atlantic meridian zone dominated by the US. As has been the thesis in this book at some length, a 'Pacific meridian' dominated by China does not represent an organic geopolitical bloc, any more than the US conception of a 'new world order.' Antipodeans in particular should hardly be expected to subjugate themselves to China. Nor is there any organic historical justification for an 'Atlantic meridian zone' of the two Americas.'

When considering the 'Eurasian' paradigm for geopolitical blocs, Dugin himself states that there must be cognisance of differences in ethnicity and religion. Moreover, if nation-states should not be based on 'artificial social constructs,' nor should geopolitical blocs being formed around new superpowers that have nothing ethnically, culturally of historically in common with the other constituents of those blocs, 'vectors' or 'meridians.' While a new concept of 'nation' and 'people' might form around a new consciousness of identity vis-à-vis a real or perceived enemy, or 'the Other,' a new geopolitical bloc might likewise be formed in terms of an alliance of states with common interests. The globalist paradigm expects states to converge into economic blocs on the basis of free trade. The thesis of this book is that new geopolitical blocs will form, even between states of disparate culture and ethnicity, on the basis of perceived threats from the two hegemonic powers, the US and China. One can see how such alliances have been formed between Russia and India and Russia and Vietnam, for example, via their common outlook on China. As crisis scenarios emerge in the Indo-Pacific, we might expect such alliances to develop into new geopolitical blocs, and as has been contended at length herein, the most desirable focus of an Indo-Pacific bloc were emerge around an indo-Russian axis.

Broader alliances with such a bloc could involve Europe via its developing relationship with Russia, an impetus being the common problems both face with Muslim militancy which, in the case of Russia, might be exploited by the US with backing for Muslim separatists in Chechnya and elsewhere. The Chechen Muslim terrorists have long received backing from the US. The self-styled Chechen Minister of Foreign Affairs, Ilyas Akhmadov, who divides his residence between the US and Britain, has received funds from the US State Department since 2004. In 2007 Putin exposed US support for Chechen terrorism as a means of dismembering Russia.[96]

As far as the US's place in a new global geopolitical orientation is concerned, this global power could implode through ethnic balkanisation. The US is held together by nothing more than a civic loyalty to a legalistic interpretation of 'patriotism,' namely the US Constitution and Bill of Rights. 'America' as a nationality has no historic depth, and a nation cannot be built around the pursuit of money, when large elements of the population will never be part of the 'American Dream.' The possibility of America's balkanisation resulting from economic collapse, has been considered by Russian Dr. Igor Panarin, professor at the Diplomatic Academy of the Russian Ministry of Foreign Affairs, who predicts, that the U.S. will break up into six parts—the Pacific coast, with its growing Chinese population; the South, with its Hispanics; Texas, where independence movements are on the rise; the Atlantic coast, with its distinct and separate mentality; five of the poorer central states with their large Native American populations; and the northern states, where the influence from Canada is strong.[97]

---

96   Webster G. Tarpley, 'Russians Blast US-UK Sponsorship of Chechen Terror,' 14 September 2007, http://tarpley.net/2007/09/14/russians-blast-us-uk-sponsorship-of-chechen-terror/.

97   'Russian Analyst Predicts Decline and Break-up of U.S.,' RIA Novosti, 24 November 2008, http://en.rian.ru/world/20081124/118512713.html.

While Panarin has been ridiculed for his prediction, and his time-frame to 2010 was really far too short, history unfolding as epochs, the broad possibilities of balkanisation, especially in regard to the large population of Hispanics in several states, who are overt in their secessionist racial (*la raza*) aims, and the de facto balkanisation across the US in terms of Black ghettoisation, make the US a tottering edifice that maintains its position through technological and military supremacy.

China's legitimate role in the world is inward, as it was for centuries. China's obsession with its superpower status via manic economic development will ensure its implosion, resulting in economic crises for states such as New Zealand, and even the US, which are dependent upon it.

'Hindustan' is accorded a special status by Dugin as a distinct civilisation, and rightly so, as historically and ethnically it is not part of Mongolian Asia. There is no commonality of interest or tradition other than where India has impressed its culture and religion further afield into the Asia region (for example, Java and Cambodia). Given these ancient historical factors, as well as the present realities of China's continued attempts at regional hegemony, in direct confrontation with India, there is no imperative historically, economically, culturally or politically for 'Hindustan' to be subsumed into a China-dominated 'Asian meridian.' Despite the simplistic Western tendency to refer to 'Asia' as though it were a geopolitical-cultural-ethnic unity, there is not nor ever has been any such concept, and there is no reason to expect such a development to occur, regardless of the pressures of outside commercial interests.

This lack of historical basis for the emergence of an 'Asian' bloc is in contrast to the 'idea of Europe,' which can be traced back to Charlemagne, having a common religion, a central axis of Pope and Emperor, the universal scholarly language of Latin, and 'outer enemies' around which a feeling of being 'European' arose, namely, those of the Mongolian and Islamic invasions, as well as Europe's crusades in the Holy Land. Hence there is an historical foundation for the prospect of a united Europe, where none has existed for 'Asia,' as a geopolitical unity.[98]

Japan attempted something of the type under the name of the 'Greater East Asia Co-Prosperity Sphere,' whose 'outer enemy' around which an Asian unity could have conceivably arisen, was the European colonial powers. This attempt of course was defeated by those powers, albeit at the cost of their own empires, and the rise in their place of the US and USSR.

Since World War II Eastern powers have arisen to dominant economic positions in the region, namely China, Japan and more latterly India. There is no concept of Asian unity other than that trying to be imposed from the *outside* in the name of commerce, centred round the US economic interests, represented publicly by the Trilateral Commission, as commented on above. There is in other words, no *inward* imperative for any such concept of an 'Asian union' in the sense of a European Union. There are antagonisms with major underlying historical, religious and cultural factors, among the Asian states, such as the antagonism and territorial disputes that exist between China and Vietnam, China and Taiwan, China and India, India and Pakistan, China and Tibet, and so on. An outward push from US and other commercial interests to form an Asian economic bloc if not an 'Asian Union' is not going to override these deep chasms. To the contrary, antagonisms are likely to reach military confrontation in the near future over resources, particularly those of water, as stated above.

---

98   Denis de Rougemont, *The Idea of Europe* (New York: Macmillan, 1966), 20. See also: Hilaire Belloc, *Europe and the Faith*, Introduction by K. R. Bolton (London: Black House Publishing, 2013).

In Dugin's system, 'Russian-Indian co-operation is the second most important meridian axis in integration on the Eurasian continent and the Eurasian collective security systems.'[99] Russia and India are natural partners, with impetus from a perceived outer threat: China.

A recent nuclear treaty with the US does not form the basis of an Indo-American alliance. Indications are that according to the terms of the treaty, US foreign policy is to place India in a dependent position on the US to counteract an Indo-Russian alignment. The treaty's clauses indicate that this is intended to hook into a relationship with the US while not offering India anything substantive to establish her security to the extent required vis-à-vis China. Hence, the treaty is designed to push India into considering the US as her 'protector' from China, in the same manner as Western Europe was pushed into the Atlantic Alliance by means of the Cold War, and again by means of a 'war on terrorism.' Ratified by US Congress on 1 October 2008, the nuclear treaty might more cynically be viewed as a means of restraining India while China has no such restraints. The treaty places India's nuclear energy development under the scrutiny of the United Nations International Atomic Energy Association (IAEA), and reaffirms India's moratorium on nuclear weapons testing. Foreign policy analysts writing for the US think tank, the Council on Foreign Relations, commented:

> India works toward negotiating a Fissile Material Cut-off Treaty (FMCT) with the United States banning the production of fissile material for weapons purposes. India agrees to prevent the spread of enrichment and reprocessing technologies to states that don't possess them and to support international non-proliferation efforts.[100]

---

99 Dugin, 'The Eurasian Idea,' 37.

100 Esther Pan and Jayshree Bajoria, 'Backgrounder: The U.S.-India Nuclear Deal,'

During US Secretary of State Hillary Clinton's trip to India in July 2009, a defence pact was signed for the expansion of US arms sales to India, including fighters and high-tech weapons. However, despite the pact and the treaty between the US and India, India's statesmen made it clear that India is not going to become an American protectorate. A far-reaching accord was also reached with Russia of very different scope than the one between India and the US.

The present relationship between Russia and India extends back to a visit by Indian Prime Minister Jawaharlal Nehru to the Soviet Union in June 1955 and Khrushchev's return trip to India in 1955. The USSR remained neutral during the border confrontations between China and India in 1959 and 1962, despite the supposedly 'fraternal relations' existing between the two nominally communist states and the 'friendship treaty' (*sic*) existing between the USSR and China.

In 1962 the Soviet Union agreed to transfer technology to co-produce the MiG-21 jet fighter in India, which the USSR had previously denied to China. Indo-Russian military cooperation is not limited to the sale of weaponry. Military cooperation extends to joint research and development, training, service to service contacts, joint naval exercises such as those that took place in April 2007 in the Sea of Japan and joint airborne exercises such as those held in September 2007 in Russia.

A few months after the aforementioned nuclear energy treaty between the US and India, in December 2008 Russia and India signed an agreement to build civilian nuclear reactors in India during a visit by the Russian president to New Delhi. This indicates India's attitude in regard to any treaty with the US as far as being wooed away from her historic relationship with Russia is concerned. Under the 'Integrated

Council on Foreign Relations, October 2008, http://www.cfr.org/publication/9663/.

Long-Term Programme of Cooperation' (ILTP) between Russia and India, India's Department of Science and Technology and Russia's Academy of Sciences and Ministry of Industry, Science and Technology are coordinated. Joint ventures under ILTP include development of SARAS Duet aircraft, semiconductor products, supercomputers, poly-vaccines, laser science and technology, seismology, high-purity materials, software and IT.

There are many other important areas of Indo-Russian cooperation, including those of space and energy. That India herself does not intend to align with the US at the expense of her relationship with Russia is indicated by her ten-year military pact with Russia formalised in October 2009. *The Hindu* reported of the pact:

The new programme of military-technical cooperation during 2011–2020 will cover both ongoing projects—such as the Su-30 MKI fighter plane and the T-90 tank production in India—as well as 31 new projects, Defence Minister A. K. Antony said. He co-chaired with Russian Defence Minister Anatoly Serdyukov the ninth session of the Indo-Russian Inter-Governmental Commission on Military Technical Cooperation (IRIGC-MTC), which met here on Wednesday and Thursday. 'It will be a bigger programme than the current 10-year programme which expires next year, and will see a further shift from the buyer-seller relationship to joint design, development and production,' Mr Antony said after the meeting.[101]

Indian Defence Minister Antony stated that the new projects under the 2020 programme would include the fifth generation fighter aircraft, the Multirole Transport Aircraft, a new multirole helicopter and many other joint

---

101 Vladimir Radyuhin, 'New 10-year Defence Tie-up with Russia Finalised,' *The Hindu*, 16 October 2009. Retrieved from: http://www.hindu.com/2009/10/16/stories/2009101659881000.htm.

projects for the Army, the Navy and the Air Force. An 'Inter-Governmental Agreement on After-Sales Product Support' would also be signed. Russia would speed up the delivery of 40 additional Su-30 MKIs commissioned by India and kits for 140 jets to be assembled in the country. 'Hitches in indigenous production of T-90 tanks in India were also resolved, Mr Antony said. Russia would expedite the construction of 140 T-90 tanks for the Indian Army and transfer of technology for production under license in India.'[102]

Indo-Russian defence ties were 'a unique partnership, as we do not have such a high-level defence cooperation arrangement with any other country,' Mr Antony told Moscow-based Indian media. 'Even as we develop cooperative ties with other countries, they will not be at the expense of our time-tested friendship with Russia.' '"The Russian side shared this perception and that was why it was willing to expand and intensify bilateral defence cooperation," Mr. Antony said.'[103] A. K. Antony's comments are a clear message to the US that Indo-Russian friendship will remain firm regardless of any accords reached with the US or its allies, and a pact clearly aimed strategically at China and China-backed Pakistan, India's only real antagonists in the region, as indicated by the comment by Serdyukov: 'I am confident the agreements reached at this session will not only guarantee the success of our military-technical cooperation but will help maintain strategic stability in the region.'[104]

Against this background of superpower rivalry and looming crises over resources, New Zealand and Australia are being forced into a China-dominated Asia on economic grounds. Vietnam and India would not accede to an Asian bloc

---

102 Ibid.

103 Ibid.

104 Ibid.

dominated by China. New Zealand and Australia, like India in the Asian sphere, constitute a separate ethnographic, cultural and economic axis, around which a Pacific bloc outside of Asia can and should develop with the south Pacific island states that are presently being wooed by China. New Zealand is for historical and ethnographic reasons intrinsically bound with Australia, and awaiting the assertion of an ANZAC axis to confront the approaching crises to the north that this writer believes will erupt most likely through rivalry over control of water.

Having established its own geopolitical axis in alliance with the South Pacific island states, an ANZAC bloc should look to India and Russia as allies on the world stage rather than to the US and China, on the basis that China represents an upcoming threat to regional security, while the US is not a reliable ally in this context at least, or would lack the will to protect New Zealand and Australia's interests vis-à-vis China. New Zealand's foreign policy, which is considered inseparable from its trade policy, is too often governed by self-righteous 'moral' considerations, rather political and geopolitical realities, let alone by any such notion as *realpolitik*, which guides nations such as the US, China and Russia. (Yet New Zealand is officially notably silent in regard to China's domination of Tibet.) Such supposedly morally-based policies and agendas as undertaken historically by others, such as 'wars against terrorism' or 'to make the world safe for democracy,' or to 'end all wars,' or for the sake of 'human rights' and so on, have served as the façade for global power politics. Not so New Zealand, whose lack of real power on the world stage is supposedly compensated for by moral outrage and posturing in regional and world forums. Hence the example of New Zealand sanctions against Fiji because the current regime does not accord with New Zealand idea's of a global liberal-democratic political model. The result of this moralising has been to open the way for Chinese influence to displace that of New Zealand,

and China is not guided by any such notions as 'political morality' as its dealings with such regimes as Mugabe's Zimbabwe and its treatment of Tibet indicate.

While the New Zealand Government expressed moral indignation at the military coup in Fiji, China's response was that, in the words of Chinese Ministry of Foreign Affairs deputy director general Deng Hongbo: 'We have always respected Fiji's status as an independent nation and we have called on the other countries to do the same and reconsider their attitudes towards Fiji and the current situation in the country.'[105] In 2007 Fiji responded to New Zealand and other Pacific Forum actions when its Finance Minister Mahendra Chaudhry stated: 'Fiji has friends in China, it has friends in Korea, it has friends in . . . other Asian countries. We're no longer relying on Australia and New Zealand.' Chaudhry added that the US had never done anything to assist Fiji.[106]

An article in the *Sydney Morning Herald* stated in 2008 that 'China's aid to Fiji has skyrocketed since the coup in December 2006.'[107] The Australian and New Zealand presence in and friendship with Fiji has consequently been eliminated, and China has become the dominant factor in Fiji's foreign relations. This extension of Chinese influence to Fiji is the latest in a long strategy to establish a dominant Chinese presence in a string of island nations throughout the Pacific and Indian oceans. As stated above, India has been the only state to respond to the Chinese naval strategy in these regions.

---

105 'China Likes to Help Developing Nations,' *Fiji Times*, 10 November 2007. Retrieved from http://www.fijitimes.

106 'Chaudhry Breaks Silence to Slag New Zealand,' Radio Nui FM, 9 July 2007. Retrieved from http://fijicoup.org/content/view/3889/.

107 Fergus Hanson, 'Don't Ignore the Big New Player in Fiji,' *Sydney Morning Herald*, 9 May 2008. Retrieved from http://www.smh.com.au/news/opinion/dont-ignore-the-big-new-player-in-fiji/2008/05/08/1210131163040.html

To New Zealand as an export-driven economy, the prospect of a Chinese market of over 1.3 billion in New Zealand's geographic region is irresistible.[108] On the other hand, it can also be pointed out that India's population is over 1.1 billion,[109] and that India also has an expanding economy. Recently New Zealand's and India's bilateral trade has increased and has much potential.[110] While the thesis of this book is that trade and economics are *not* the foundations for genuine alliances, for these states they represent an increased consciousness of one another, and importantly also, prompt New Zealand to look to another market beyond China, and one moreover that does not have hegemonic designs. Additionally there are trade negotiations taking place with Russia.

Ideally, an emerging Indo-Pacific bloc with an Indo-Russian nexus would leave the world trade system and seek to become autarchic, and undertake bilateral barter. Only by a reorientation of the trading system can there be genuine resistance to globalisation. Such a possibility is not beyond reality: Thailand has a barter deal with Russia to exchange rice for four Mi-17 helicopters.[111] In 1991 Russia initiated barter with Poland, exchanging crude oil and natural gas for grain and other agricultural products.[112] If Russia truly wants to be free of 'oligarchs,' not only in Russia but worldwide, then barter is a necessity to bypass the globalist economic system.

---

108 World Bank World Development Indicators, 2008. Retrieved from http://www. google.com/publicdata?ds=wbwdi&met=sp_pop_totl&idim=country:CHN&q=chi na%27s+population#met=sp_pop_totl&idim=country:CHN.

109 Ibid.

110 Ruth Le Pla, 'Increased Trade Between India and New Zealand a Real Possibility,' 14 February 2013, http://www.asianz.org.nz/node/4697.

111 'Thailand to Acquire Chinese, Russian weaponry in Barter Deals,' *Barter News*, http://www.barternews.com/thailand_acquires_chinese_russian_weaponry_in_ barter_deals.htm.

112 William Engdahl, 'Polish-Russian Barter Deal Sets Model for Trade East,' *EIR News*, vol. 18, no. 6, 20 September 1991, 4.

China has been developing relations, especially through aid with Tonga, Nauru, Papua New Guinea, Vanuatu and as stated Fiji. In 2007 China issued a White Paper that demarcated 'first and second lines of island defence' in the Pacific as China's spheres of influence. The first line of defence runs from Taiwan through to the disputed Spratly Islands to Singapore. The second island-chains describe the sphere of influence that China expects to achieve in the Pacific Ocean. According to the White Paper, China plans to upgrade its navy to control 'what its military calls the "first-island chain" by 2010 and to the "second-island chain" by 2040.' The 'first-island chain' includes Japan, Taiwan, the Philippines and Brunei. The second-island chain extends to Australia.[113]

New Zealand and Australian politicians only see trade in such relations; China sees geopolitical aims as shown by the reference to a 'political role in the region.' There have been a few isolated, authoritative voices warning about the geopolitical consequences of China's incursion into this region. Captain Kuli Taumoefolau, the former commander of the Tongan Defence Service training, operations and intelligence unit, stated during hearings on New Zealand's relationship with Tonga, 'Don't underestimate, never underestimate China.' A TVNZ News report stated of Captain Taumoefolau that he was worried about China's growing influence in the Pacific. 'Taumoefolau says New Zealand should strengthen its own military ties with Tonga to counter China's growing influence in the Pacific.'[114] Political scientist Paul Buchanan of Auckland University, a defence specialist who has served as a consultant for the CIA, expressed his own concerns. Both received scant attention from the news media. Buchanan was quoted in the same report as stating that the Pacific is the playground

---

113   Phil Brennan, 'China Rebuilds Its Military Muscle,' *NewsMax*, 19 October 2002. Retrieved from http://archive.

114   'NZ Warned of Chinese Influence,' *TVNZ News*, 17 June 2004.

where superpowers test their rivalries. Buchanan, in a reply to questions from this writer, stated:

. . . My take is that the People's Republic of China (PRC) is the next superpower, and could well eclipse the USA by mid-century. It currently consumes the second largest amount of petroleum in the world, has the second largest military expenditures in the world, is growing at 9 per cent per year, has no former colonies or imperialist attachments to worry about other than Taiwan, and is not involved in the military conflicts of the moment.

The US is starting to feel the pressure, which makes the PRC its major long-term strategic problem. For its part, as part of asserting its emergence, the PRC is establishing a forward presence in the Western Pacific, which is the natural avenue for it to project blue water force and pursue commercial interests (fisheries) outside the South China Sea. Plus help ensure the safety of its oil shipments from the Middle East, which all have to pass through the Straits of Molluca.

It may well be the beginning of a new balance of power in the region, although the US Pacific Fleet contingency plans for that eventuality. NZ should also plan for the new geo-strategic realities that the expanding presence of the PRC entails. Anyway, that is a brief synopsis of a somewhat longer conversation I had with the reporter.[115]

Such views, however authoritative, do not carry any weight with New Zealand's political and business interests intent on pursuing attachments with China regardless of the long-term consequences for the region. Indeed, already Sino-New Zealand relations have begun extending into the military field. In 2008 the official China news agency Xinhua

115 Dr. Paul Buchanan, personal communication to K. R. Bolton, 18 June 2004.

reported on a high level meeting between the Chinese and New Zealand militaries. To this writer's knowledge no New Zealand news media reported this. China's news agency Xinhua reported:

> BEIJING, 4 July (Xinhua)—China and New Zealand vowed here on Friday to further army exchanges to push forward military relations between the two countries.
>
> 'The Chinese armed forces advocate expanding contact and substantial cooperation with their New Zealand counterparts to upgrade military relations in the long run,' said Chen Bingde, chief of the General Staff of the Chinese People's Liberation Army. During a meeting with New Zealand army chief Louis Gardiner, Chen hailed the relationship between China and New Zealand, saying it conformed to the fundamental interests of the two countries and peoples and contributed to regional peace and prosperity.
>
> 'Gardiner said the military ties between New Zealand and China had maintained sustainable development and cooperation kept improving, adding that New Zealand would continue to enhance cooperation and exchanges with China and its military.'[116]

An ANZAC bloc as a sovereign geopolitical entity if brought out from under the control of foreign capital and permitted to self-develop would, like a self-developed European Union, or a 'Bolivarian' bloc, possess vast potential resources and the freedom to develop alliances with states based on genuine geopolitical and ethnographic considerations rather than being pushed by globalist economics. To paraphrase Charles de Gaulle: 'We don't have friends, only interests.'

---

116 'China, New Zealand Pledge to Further Army Exchanges,' *Chinaview*, 9 July 2008. Retrieved from www.chinaview.cn.

How realistic is the proposition of an ANZAC alliance, which moreover reorientates its foreign policy towards India and Russia and other states in the region (such as Vietnam and Taiwan) in the face of Chinese expansion, and against the background of a coming rivalry for resources? Statesmen are starting to think geopolitically in terms of vast expanses, in an era where the nation-state is becoming obsolete. While between the US and its allies this geopolitical thinking takes the form of globalisation and a 'new world order,' others of significance are thinking of alternatives to the liberal economic model of globalisation.

Some European thinkers, such as Dr. Olivier Védrine, are reviving the ideal of President Charles de Gaulle of a Europe from the Atlantic to the Urals, similar to the concept of 'Eurasianism' revived by Dugin which has many adherents among political, economic and military elites not only in Russia but as far as Turkey.[117] In the Americas, while the political and business elite push for such globalising tendencies as NAFTA, some Latin American states, centred around Venezuela, are working towards an alternative Latin American geopolitical bloc.

Therefore geopolitical alternatives to the liberal-economic free trade model of globalisation are now being discussed in some prominent places throughout the world. If the crisis scenarios that this writer has discussed unfold over the course of the next few decades, Australia and New Zealand might be required by force of outside circumstances to look to an ANZAC bloc as a means of trying to become insulated from the upheavals that Asia could face. In this scenario Russia and India cannot be ignored. Chinese intransigence over both territorial claims and resources will form what can be called the 'outer enemy,' which has historically welded peoples, nations and cultures together into alliances and geopolitical blocs.

---

117 Dugin, op. cit., 37–38.

Conclusion

India stands on the frontline of world-historical changes. New Zealand feels insulated by distance, but seeks closeness to Asia via trade, the primary determinant of its foreign and economic policies. Indians and Russians in academia and government understand very much more about world historical realities. India still shrewdly rejects US overtures and blandishments, while maintaining and indeed expanding her traditional relations with Russia. Despite the supposed bloc that is identified as 'BRIC,' India and Russia both remain wary of China and although trade and diplomacy proceeds, India's policy-makers and military leaders at least are not so naïve as to let their guard down.

China functions in symbiosis with US and other Western businesses, and there is no real conflict of interests. Indeed, the US functions economically courtesy of China. In any Indo-Pacific conflict, the US will not confront China. Indeed, policy-makers and businessmen see China as a partner in the 'brave new world' to the degree that Russia could never be. India is the added factor in the geopolitical equation: full of potential but in need of radical transformations to fulfil that potential.

Nations often do not become conscious of their identity or destiny until placed in confrontation. They come to self-consciousness most readily vis-à-vis 'the Other.' While there is no such geopolitical, ethnographic or historical basis to the economic construct named 'Asia,' new blocs within Asia and embracing the entirety of the Indo-Pacific region can—and in terms of survival—must emerge. My contention is that for the Indo-Pacific to resist the hegemonic ambitions of both the US and China, the lead can only come from India and Russia. The implications are beyond the region, however, and are world-embracing. The future will belong to geopolitical blocs, or what the Russian geopolitical theorist Alexander Dugin calls 'vectors,' rather than the 'new world order' envisaged by the US immediately after the implosion of the Soviet bloc.

About the Author

Kerry R. Bolton is a Fellow of the Institute of Higher Studies on Geopolitics and Auxiliary Sciences (Lisbon) and of the Academy of Social and Political Research (Athens), assisting with the editing of the Academy's scholarly journal *Ab Aeterno*. He is a contributing writer for *Foreign Policy Journal*, and has been widely published by the scholarly and broader media, including *Geopolitica* (Moscow State University); *International Journal of Social Economics*; *Journal of Social, Political and Economic Studies*; *Antrocom Journal of Anthropology*; *International Journal of Russian Studies*; etc., and the Indian journals *World Affairs*, *India Quarterly*, *The Great Indian Dream*, and *Bureaucracy Today*. His books include *Revolution from Above* (2011), *Artists of the Right* (2012), *The Parihaka Cult* (2012), *Stalin: The Enduring Legacy* (2012), *The Psychotic Left* (2013), and *The Banking Swindle* (2013). He lives with his wife on the Kapiti Coast, New Zealand.

www.ingramcontent.com/pod-product-compliance
Lightning Source LLC
Chambersburg PA
CBHW070912270326
41927CB00011B/2542